First Steps in Counselling

A Students' Companion for Basic Introductory Courses

Pete Sanders

PCCS BOOKS
Manchester

First Published in 1994
Reprinted 1994

PCCS BOOKS
Paragon House
48 Seymour Grove
Manchester
M16 0LN
Tel (0161) 877 9877

First Steps in Counselling - A Students' Companion for Basic Introductory Courses

ISBN 1 898059 05 5

Cover design by Peter Kneebone
Printed by Printoff Graphic Arts Ltd. Alexander House,
Lomeshaye Road, Nelson, Lancashire.

Contents

Acknowledgements

The author and PCCS would like to thank the following publishers and authors for their kind permission to use the copyright material listed below.

Song Lyrics
ONCE IN A LIFETIME
Words and Music by DAVID BYRNE, CHRIS FRANTZ, TINA WEYMOUTH, JERRY HARRISON and BRIAN ENO.
(C) 1982 EG Music Ltd/co-publisher notice (provided by Warner Chappell Music Ltd) for the world. All Rights reserved.
(C) 1992 Index Music Inc/Bleu Disque Music Co Inc, USA. Warner Chappell Music Ltd, London W1Y 3FA
HUMAN BEHAVIOUR
Words and Music by NELLEE HOOPER, ANTONIO CARLOS JOBIM and BJORK GUDMUNDSDOTTIR
(C) 1993 Ensign Music Corp/Gudmundsdottir Designee/Famous Music Corp, USA
Warner Chappell Music Ltd, London W1Y 3FA. And Polygram Music Ltd.
I AM AFRAID
Words and music by DAVID COUSE. Reproduced by kind permission of Chrysalis Music Ltd.
BOYS DON'T CRY
THE CURE lyrics used with kind permission from Fiction Songs Ltd, London W1P 1LB.

Books
Claude Bristol, (1985) *The Magic of Believing,* a Fireside book published by Simon & Schuster.
British Association for Counselling, (1991) *Definition of Terms in Use with Expansion and Rationale.*
Dryden, W. and Spurling, L. Eds (1989) *On Becoming a Psychotherapist,* London: Routledge.
Eysenck, H.J. (1953) *Uses and Abuses of Psychology,* Penguin Books Ltd.
Marilyn Ferguson, (1981) *The Aquarian Conspiracy,* Routledge.
Friends, Religious Society of *Questions & Counsel,* London Yearly Meeting 1988 No16.
Hannah Green, (1972) *I never Promised You a Rose Garden,* Pan. (1964 Gollancz)
Russell Hoban, (1975) *Turtle Diary,* Picador, published by Pan Books.
Edgar N. Jackson, (1978) *The Many Faces of Grief,* SCM
Jung, C.G. (1954) *The Practice of Psychotherapy* Vol 16 of The Collected Works. London: Routledge & Keegan Paul.
Maeder, Thomas. (1989) *Children of Psychiatrists and Other Psychotherapists,* New York: Harper & Row
Ann Oakley, (1985) *Taking it Like a Woman,* Flamingo (Fontana Paperbacks)
Boris Pasternak, (1988) *Doctor Zhivago,* Harper Collins.
Carl Rogers, (1961) *On Becoming a Person,* Constable.
Carl Rogers, (1978) *Carl Rogers On Personal Power - Inner strength and its revolutionary impact,* Constable.
Natalie Rogers, (1980) *Emerging Woman - A Decade of Midlife Transitions.* Santa Rosa: Personal Press.
Janice Russell, Graham Dexter and Tim Bond (1992) *Differentiation Between Advice, Guidance, Befriending, Counselling Skills and Counselling,* Advice, Guidance and Counselling Lead Body.
Paul Tournier, (1978) *The Violence Inside,* tr Eward Hudson. SCM.
Morris West, (1963) *Shoes of The Fisherman,* Heinemann.
Winnicott, D.W., (1971) *Therapeutic Consultations in Child Psychiatry,* London: Hogarth Press.

Introduction
(Read this first)

When I started writing this book it seemed a good idea to produce a book for students on introductory courses, since I could find precious few books written for this group of students. I think I now know why.

A very broad spectrum of people come to introductory counselling courses for a wide variety of reasons. Trying to write something that would be a useful and rewarding read for the majority has proved challenging and taxing. I realise that some course participants will have no prior knowledge or experience of counselling, whilst others may have come across counselling before, or may even be doing it as a volunteer or as part of their job.

I have tried hard to pitch the book so that it is a 'catch-all' with something for everyone on introductory courses whatever their starting point. In attempting this, I realised that three things would need to be made clear; firstly that the book is not trying to teach or train standing alone, but is intended as a supplement to a course, a 'course text' if you like. Secondly that the course level aimed at is below counselling skills courses, they would need a different type of book. Finally that the key themes of the book are *information* and *self-awareness*.

I am not the first to suggest that personal development is achieved via many routes and that our ideas in counselling come from many different sources. It is as if to underline this, for the benefit of beginning helpers right from the start, that I decided to include quotes from a wide range of sources. The quotes are ones that have special meaning for me and it would be a bonus if they strike a chord with some readers too. I've included quotes from pop songs to illustrate the fact that personal development and counselling values crop up all over the place. Every now and then I hear a song that makes the hairs stand up on the back of my neck. If you are not familiar with these songs and would like to listen to them, the sources (records and CDs) are listed in the References section, although I'm still some way off having 'First Steps in Counselling - The Album'.

I have felt for some time that the participants on introductory courses are a very influential group. Not only are they the seed corn for certificate and diploma courses, but even if they do not proceed any further with their counselling training, they carry away with them a view of counselling. This view of counselling will be passed on to friends, relatives, colleagues, or the person standing in the pub. These participants whose introductory course experience is their one and only contact with counselling will pass judgement on counselling on the basis of this contact. My aim with this book is to help make that judgement as well-informed and positive towards the value of counselling as possible.

None of the chapters in this book is complete. It is in the nature of helping and counselling to be a process moving towards something rather than arriving at a state of completion. I have tried to raise as many issues as possible through the examples in the book, issues which I make no attempt to resolve. It is for the course tutors to decide how best to work with them.

Finally I would like to thank a number of people for helping me with this book at various stages, to Maggie for her support and proofreading. Thanks also to Alan Frankland for his helpful and sensitive comments on various bits of the book. Much of the book makes more sense thanks to Alan. Finally, thanks to the participants on my introductory courses over the past 12 months whose ideas and comments have found their way onto the 'flipcharts' in the book. The imaginary groups are actually mixtures of comments and ideas from a number of introductory course groups.

If I could dedicate this book to anyone it would be dedicated to the trainers at Off The Record Tyneside circa 1972 - 4. They helped me take my own first steps in counselling.

Pete Sanders
Manchester 1994

What is Counselling?

1

Introductions - Who are you?

Most introductory courses in counselling begin with an activity where each person in the group has to introduce themselves to the rest of the group. Sometimes the activity is made a little more complicated and you will be asked to choose another person in the group to pair up with and talk to for a minute or two. Then you will be asked to introduce your partner to the rest of the group.

This can be quite a challenge if you're not used to speaking in groups, especially if you feel a little awkward talking about yourself. Counselling training is a challenging business, so most courses start as they mean to continue! Also, it's important for you to get to know each other reasonably well so that you can feel relaxed about talking in the group. Most of the learning in Introductory Courses happens through the process of sharing your ideas with others and listening to what they have to say. The listening bit here is important, since nearly everyone would agree that it is a skill which lies at the very heart of counselling, so the more we practise the better.

Would you like to introduce yourself now? It's just as true for this book as it is for your counselling course group - if we can form a relationship through the pages of this book, it will be all the easier for me to write and you to read. So, who are you, and how would you introduce yourself to me, what kind of information would you include?

As for me, my name is Pete Sanders. I decided to call myself 'Pete' rather than 'Peter' when I was 17 and still at school after reading a book on numerology. I worked out that according to the system in the book, 'Pete Sanders' added up to a number with better star potential than 'Peter Sanders'.

I am married to Maggie, my second wife (I am her second husband). Between us we have four children, one of mine and one of hers live with us the others live with their mum and dad in Birmingham and London respectively.

I got involved in counselling by accident when I was an undergraduate student in Newcastle-upon-Tyne in 1972. I joined a phone-in and drop-in youth counselling agency called 'Off the Record' as a volunteer and decided that I wanted to do counselling as a job. I went to Aston University and completed the Diploma in Counselling in Educational settings Course in 1975. I went from there to work as a counsellor and lecturer in Further Education Colleges until I took voluntary redundancy in 1993 to go freelance.

'Spare' or 'leisure' time for me has become a rather curious concept since I gave up my previous job working in a college. Maggie gave up her job as a teacher at the same time and we both now work from home which means we see a lot of each other. So far that's great and we both enjoy just wandering into the garden when we choose to pull up a weed or two.

Now I've introduced myself, I'm wondering why I chose the bits of my life that I did. I deliberately put in the things that I thought you might be interested in and wanted to keep it brief so that you didn't get bored or think that I was showing off.

What about you? Did you think of 'who you are' in terms of your family and home life? Your hobbies and the things you enjoy? Or work related things like the job you do or whether you are in employment? Which are the most important, the most acceptable, and which would you choose to tell me? Which are the most private and which would you choose not to tell me?

How do these questions sound to you at this stage? Perhaps you feel puzzled by them, worried by them or pleased to be asked them. Counselling training tends to emphasise feelings more than other subjects, so you will find more of this as we go along.

Expectations - Why are you reading this?
There are few courses of study that do *not* start with the tutor asking some or all of the students why they have chosen to study that particular subject. There can be few books, however, which begin by asking the reader why they've chosen to read it. Something, or someone, has brought counselling and you together so-to-speak. This book is intended to be your companion on an exciting journey of discovery. When you see this symbol:

✍ *MAKE A NOTE OF YOUR OWN ANSWERS & EXAMPLES*

On this journey you will find the answers to some important questions which will help you decide whether you really do want to pursue this interest in

counselling any further. Questions such as:
- Why am I interested in counselling?
- What got me interested in this course?
- What do I think counselling is?
- What do I hope will come of it?
- What are my fears about this course?
- What will be expected of me - what are the demands of counselling?
- Will I be up to it?

It may take some time before you feel satisfied that you can answer these questions fully, but now is a good place to start. The answers will be found over the duration of your introductory course by:
- Finding out more about *what counselling is*, and
- Finding out more about *yourself*.

You may be wondering why finding out more about yourself and your motives is so important. Chapter 3 on 'The Importance of Self-Development' will look in some detail at this issue.

Definitions of Counselling
After the introductions and getting us to ask ourselves why we've chosen to learn about counselling, it's a good idea to move on to looking at what counselling is. This question usually reveals the variety of ideas, attitudes and opinions regarding counselling, what it is, who it's for and who should be doing it. This isn't surprising since counselling has risen from almost total obscurity to the word on nearly everyone's lips in the past ten years. In that time there have been some brave attempts to arrive at a definition, but people will keep on using it to describe so many different activities!

- In educational settings, 'counselling' is used alongside the term guidance, often to mean helping people find the right course or job.

• In medical settings and the armed forces some people use 'counselling' in an old fashioned way to mean discipline. If you have been 'counselled' it means you have been told off or warned that some misdemeanour will go on your record.

• The phrase 'debt counselling' is now used to describe the help you can get to arrange your finances by making regular payments and budgeting.

• Some agencies use the term 'counselling' to describe information and advice given on a particular topic, a healthcare issue perhaps such as family planning or safe sex.

• Many people use 'counselling' to mean any kind of helping activity that they do that hasn't got another more commonplace name like 'tutoring' in education, or 'treatment' in medicine.

So, what do you think? *Just what is counselling?* What happens to you when you see or hear the word?
   • What **images** does the word conjure up for you?
   • **Who** do you think of?
   • What **sounds** do you hear?
   • What **thoughts** come into your mind?
   • What **feelings** do you have?

Where do these ideas, feelings sounds and images come from?
   • Personal experience of being counselled?
   • The beliefs of friends and family?
   • What you've read in the papers or seen on TV?
   • Someone you know who is a counsellor?
   • Books about counselling or psychology?
   • Other books, e.g. novels or books about health or spiritual matters?

'People become engaged in counselling when a person, occupying regularly or temporarily the role of counsellor offers or agrees explicitly to offer time, attention and respect to another person or persons temporarily in the role of client.

The task of counselling is to give the client an opportunity to explore, discover and clarify ways of living more resourcefully and towards greater well-being.'

Counselling: Definition of Terms in Use with Expansion and Rationale. British Association for Counselling (1991).

'Counselling is an activity freely entered into by the person seeking help, it offers the opportunity to identify things for the client themselves that are troubling or perplexing. It is clearly and explicitly contracted, and the boundaries of the relationship identified. The activity itself is designed to help self exploration and understanding. The process should help to identify thoughts, emotions and behaviours that, once accessed, may offer the client a greater sense of personal resources and self determined change.'

Differentiation Between Advice, Guidance, Befriending, Counselling Skills and Counselling. Janice Russell, Graham Dexter and Tim Bond, (1992). Advice, Guidance and Counselling Lead Body.

As you set out on this journey of discovery, it might be useful to write down your answers to these questions. It would be interesting to look at them again at the end of the course to see if and/or how your views have changed. ✍

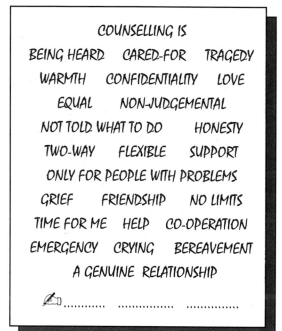

The flip chart above shows some possible responses from a hypothetical training group on an introductory course (the blank spaces leave room for other ideas). How do they compare with the thoughts and feelings you came up with? Each phrase says something about a person's view of counselling, what it is and what it means to them. Let's look at some in a little more detail to find out what people mean by these words.

BEING HEARD Means being **really heard**. It feels as though the other person is **really interested** in me, and is trying to **understand**.

WARMTH This is when I feel **welcomed** by someone. As if they're pleased to see me and **really mean it**. It seems as though they genuinely like me.

CONFIDENTIALITY This is very important if I'm to feel safe. I must be sure that the other person **isn't going to tell anyone else** about what I've said, or even that I've been to see them, in case it's embarrassing.

EQUAL I like to feel I'm on an equal footing with the other person. So that they're **not acting in a superior way** like an 'expert' or have any power over me.

NON-JUDGEMENTAL I don't like the feeling of being judged or told off. Some people make me feel as though I've done wrong by the way they speak to me. I prefer to **feel accepted** as a person, then I feel safe.

ONLY FOR PEOPLE WITH PROBLEMS Counselling is for people with problems, e.g. marriage guidance. I don't have problems so I don't need to see a counsellor.

NO LIMITS If I go to a counsellor I should be able to talk about **anything at all** that I think is important.

CRYING It's OK to cry when you're upset, e.g. if someone close to you has died. Counselling should help you **express your feelings**.

RELATIONSHIP Counselling is a helping relationship, a caring relationship. It's about what happens **between two people**.

Having looked in more detail at some of the meanings behind the 'key words' on the flipchart, do you agree or disagree? (Remember that these are the fictitious views of an imaginary group.)

I have found it helpful to look at counselling in comparison to other helping roles and activities to see where the boundaries are between counselling and the rest of everyday life. Most of us are familiar with the roles of Parent, Friend and Doctor. By this I mean that we have experience of being a patient visiting the doctor, of being a son or daughter (and perhaps a parent) and of being someone's friend. What do we want from people in these roles and what to we try to offer when we are in these roles? They are all helpers of one sort or another, so it's clear that helping comes in many different colours. (You could also try other helping roles such as teacher, nurse, priest etc.)

Here are some more flipcharts with ideas from our hypothetical group:

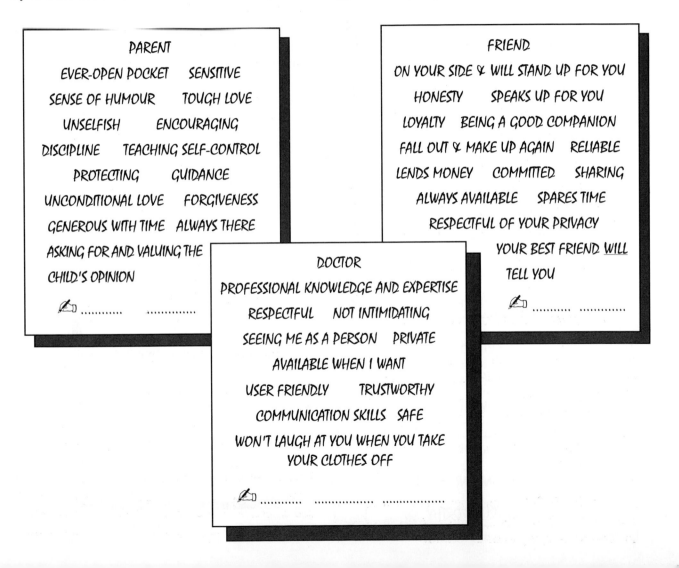

PARENT

EVER-OPEN POCKET   SENSITIVE

SENSE OF HUMOUR   TOUGH LOVE

UNSELFISH   ENCOURAGING

DISCIPLINE   TEACHING SELF-CONTROL

PROTECTING   GUIDANCE

UNCONDITIONAL LOVE   FORGIVENESS

GENEROUS WITH TIME   ALWAYS THERE

ASKING FOR AND VALUING THE

CHILD'S OPINION

....

FRIEND

ON YOUR SIDE & WILL STAND UP FOR YOU

HONESTY   SPEAKS UP FOR YOU

LOYALTY   BEING A GOOD COMPANION

FALL OUT & MAKE UP AGAIN   RELIABLE

LENDS MONEY   COMMITTED   SHARING

ALWAYS AVAILABLE   SPARES TIME

RESPECTFUL OF YOUR PRIVACY

YOUR BEST FRIEND WILL

TELL YOU

....

DOCTOR

PROFESSIONAL KNOWLEDGE AND EXPERTISE

RESPECTFUL   NOT INTIMIDATING

SEEING ME AS A PERSON   PRIVATE

AVAILABLE WHEN I WANT

USER FRIENDLY   TRUSTWORTHY

COMMUNICATION SKILLS SAFE

WON'T LAUGH AT YOU WHEN YOU TAKE

YOUR CLOTHES OFF

....

How do your thoughts about these helping roles fit in with the flipcharts above? These roles represent the ways of helping and caring that are commonplace in our culture and that we've probably grown up with. Our ideas about good caring tell us a lot about ourselves and it seems as though there might be some common themes about helping which are shared by these roles. This activity also helps us understand where counselling-style helping begins and ends, where it overlaps with other helping activities and where it's different. These limits are called *boundaries*.

Boundaries between Counselling and Other Ways of Helping.

Boundaries help define an activity by creating a **space** within which the activity can take place. 'Space' brings to mind *my* space, *safe* space, *open* space, *sacred* space, the client's space. In order to make the counselling space safe for the client we protect it with boundaries. These boundaries will keep certain non-counselling or worldly things out and certain counselling-style helping things in.

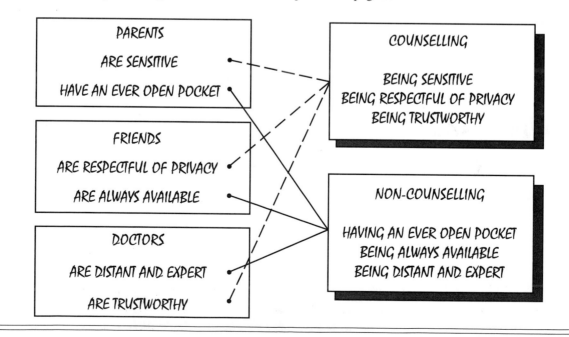

Counselling and Non-Counselling Ways of Helping

Some ways of helping in our culture are fine as counselling ways of helping. On the other hand, some perfectly good ways of helping as a friend, parent, or doctor would be no good as counselling ways of helping. For example , taking some items from our flipcharts on page 5:

PARENTS
ARE SENSITIVE
HAVE AN EVER OPEN POCKET

FRIENDS
ARE RESPECTFUL OF PRIVACY
ARE ALWAYS AVAILABLE

DOCTORS
ARE DISTANT AND EXPERT
ARE TRUSTWORTHY

COUNSELLING
BEING SENSITIVE
BEING RESPECTFUL OF PRIVACY
BEING TRUSTWORTHY

NON-COUNSELLING
HAVING AN EVER OPEN POCKET
BEING ALWAYS AVAILABLE
BEING DISTANT AND EXPERT

> The wise ruler says:
> I take no action and the people are transformed of themselves;
> I prefer stillness and the people are rectified of themselves;
> I do not interfere and the people prosper of themselves;
> I am free from desire and the people of themselves become simple like the uncarved block.
> Lao Tzu: *Tao te Ching*, LXXIII.179
>
>
> 'Look here,' Furii said. 'I never promised you a rose-garden. I never promised you perfect justice...and I never promised you peace or happiness. My help is so that you can be free to fight for all these things. The only reality I offer is challenge, and being well is being free to accept it or not at whatever level you are capable. I never promise lies, and the rose-garden world of perfection is a lie - and a bore too!'
> Hannah Green: *I Never Promised You a Rose Garden*. p. 101

As can be seen in the panel opposite, some ways of helping are role or context specific. It would not be appropriate for a counsellor to lend clients money or be constantly available for them. The boundary between what counselling is and what it is not has been, and is currently the subject of serious debate.

The debate is being held by the Advice, Guidance Counselling and Psychotherapy Lead Body, who are responsible for eventually agreeing a set of competencies for counselling so that qualifications in counselling can be standardised. Their first task is to identify what counselling is and how it is different from other forms of helping such as befriending, guidance, advice etc.

They are also interested in another distinction which is seen as important in counselling circles. The distinction between *using counselling skills* and *being a counsellor*. It may never have occurred to you to separate these two activities before, but the distinction is seen as important.

Using Counselling Skills

Counselling skills can be used by anyone either as a separate set of techniques or, more usually, as a set of skills either integrated with, or alongside, an already well established set of professional or 'people' skills. In such a case we might find:

- a nurse using counselling skills when he listens to a patient or comforts grieving relatives.
- a teacher using counselling skills when she is told by a school pupil that he is being bullied.
- a manager using counselling skills when an employee tell her that he is thinking of quitting work to look after an ageing parent.
- a person working at home to bring up children might use counselling skills to comfort a neighbour when their spouse is made redundant.
- a colleague listening really well in order to resolve a disagreement in a meeting.

You might have chosen to attend a basic counselling course to help you in a similar setting at your place of work or in the community. We will look at *who counselling is for* in more detail in Chapter 9.

My own definition of counselling skills is:

Counselling skills are interpersonal communication skills derived from the study of therapeutic change in human beings, used in a manner consistent with the goals and values of the established ethics of the profession of the practitioner in question. In addition, the user of counselling skills will find that their own professional skills are enhanced by the process.

Pete Sanders: *An Incomplete Guide to Using Counselling Skills on The Telephone,* p 19.

Counselling

There are many different ways of understanding the nature of counselling. It can be seen as:
• a **counselling approach** to people, i.e. a way of *understanding or looking* at caring for and helping our fellow humans,
• a set of **counselling skills**, i.e. some ways of *behaving* in a caring way,
• a set of **counselling goals** or caring and helping *aims* which we are hoping to achieve.

Some other ways of helping may share some of these features, but not all. When you have all three of the above, then you have counselling.

Definitions of Non-Counselling Helping

Guidance

To offer a confidential, accountable service which helps the client to develop self awareness. To enable the client to be aware of and have access to accurate, appropriate information on available opportunities in order to make informed choices. The client is offered opportunities to explore relevant concerns and to develop decision making skills. The activity is designed to help the management of transition appropriate to the client's needs and wishes.

Advice

Advising enables the client to solve problems and make decisions by offering accurate, current and appropriate information. It seeks to widen the client's choice by informing them of their rights, options and possible action programmes.

Befriending

To provide ongoing quality support to distressed individuals for an indeterminate period of time. The activity should enable appropriate, realistic and healthy coping skills to be developed in a warm and trusting relationship. Befriending is intended to lessen the person's sense of social or personal isolation.

Differentiation Between Advice, Guidance, Befriending, Counselling Skills and Counselling, Janice Russell, Graham Dexter, Tim Bond, (1992) Advice, Guidance and Counselling Lead Body.

Helping in a counselling way may share a counselling approach to helping and some of the goals, for example. When using counselling skills, we may share the counselling skills but have a different approach and different goals, e.g. using counselling skills in a nursing setting to achieve nursing goals.

A slightly different way of looking at the problem is to see the definition of counselling as dependent upon the *boundaries of the activity,* the *qualities of the relationship*, and the *aims or functions of the activity.*

The essential **boundaries** of counselling are:
- That it is practised by someone designated as a counsellor.
- That the counsellor be appropriately trained to be able to practise to an acceptable standard.
- That the counsellor abides by a code of ethics and practice*.
- That the client knows that the service being offered by the counsellor is counselling.

*One of the key differences between counselling and using counselling skills is that the counsellor is bound by a code of ethics and practice, and carries a set of professional responsibilities. When using counselling skills, you are governed by another set of ethical principles and professional responsibilities, e.g. nursing or teaching.

The essential **qualities** of the relationship are:
- That the counsellor shows deep respect for the client.
- The counsellor and client will agree on what the relationship will set out to achieve and how it will seek to achieve it✿.

- That the client will feel safe enough to be challenged.
- That the client will feel valued as a person.
- The counsellor does not judge the client.

✿Another of the key differences between counselling and the use of counselling skills, is that the counsellor and client will make an agreement regarding what the client wants from the counsellor and what the counsellor is prepared to offer.

The **aims** or **functions** of counselling are:
- That the client will feel empowered (i.e. have a greater sense of personal autonomy).
- The client has a greater sense of self-understanding.
- To enable the client to live in a more 'satisfying and resourceful way'. (See Russell et al 1992).
- That the client has a greater sense of well-being.
- That the above 'gains' should be enduring.

Hopefully the elements of the definitions above will find agreement amongst a wide range of counsellors. As you can see from the various quotations in the bold edged boxes, there is a general convergence of views on what counselling actually is, albeit expressed in slightly different ways.

How do the various definitions and elements of definitions we have looked at compare with your own ideas?

✍

What counselling is not

As this introductory chapter has progressed, we have looked both at what counselling is and what counselling is not.

Counselling is not:
> Being a friend.
> Caring in a parental way.
> 'Treating' or 'healing' someone like a doctor.
> Instructing or teaching.
> Advising.
> Giving guidance.
> Just using counselling skills.

Sometimes we can find counselling difficult to do well and when we begin to find it difficult we tend to revert back to a way of helping which is more familiar to us.
> •The chances are that *you* will prefer to help in a particular way or style. Perhaps because of your job, or maybe because of your personality, you tend to help in a *'teaching'* style or a *'parental'* style or a *'friendly'* style etc.

Others take the view that counselling is potentially a very 'natural' helping style for us as long as we can *stop* trying to do something else like taking control of the situation, thinking we know best, or judging the person we are trying to help.
> • What tendencies do you have to rescue, judge or take control when you are trying to help in a counselling way?

Throughout your basic introductory course you will get feedback from your fellow students and tutors. Some of this feedback might concern what they experience of your natural style of helping. It will be useful to take note of this so that you can identify those occasions when you feel most tempted to stop a counselling style and revert to your natural style. When this happens you have a choice between two styles of helping, both useful under different circumstances. How should this choice be exercised?

• Your children might generally prefer you to help them in a parent-like way rather than be a counsellor.
> *Would it be appropriate to offer them counselling-style helping under some circumstances?*

• People in a client role might prefer you to help them in a counselling way.
> *Would it be appropriate to offer them help in a parental style, teaching style friendly style or healing style under some circumstances?*

Each way of helping is fine under the right circumstances. Counselling, using counselling skills and helping in a counselling way are no better or worse that other ways of helping, just different and suited to certain circumstances. People seeking help have the right to ask for a helping style that suits them, however, we are under no obligation to provide a helping style that we don't feel comfortable with.

There are few of us for whom a counselling way of helping is easy the first time we try to do it, even though we think it is 'right' for us because it is in harmony with our values. We need to practise and work at it at a number of levels; our self awareness, our knowledge and our skills. The remaining chapters in the book look in more detail at each of these at a level appropriate to an introductory course.

Counselling or Psychotherapy?

I have made some effort to come to some helpful definitions in this first chapter, but the truth is that the whole area of professional counselling and psychotherapy is still rather ill defined in this country. One of the most frequently asked questions is 'What is the difference between counselling and psychotherapy?' Worse still from a public relations point of view, I cannot say that there is an answer on which most professionals can agree.

The British Association for Counselling (BAC) had a keynote speech by Brian Thorne at its 1992 Annual Conference with the title '**Psychotherapy and Counselling: The Quest for Differences**' (published in *Counselling* Vol.3 No.4 December 1992). At the 1993 Annual General Meeting the BAC debated whether it should embrace the word 'psychotherapy' in its title. So you can see that even in professional circles it is a matter for debate. Some would say that the debate is about professional status or even control of the psychological side of the helping professions.

The BAC Code of Ethics and Practice says on the subject:

> 'It is not possible to make a generally accepted distinction between counselling and psychotherapy. There are well founded traditions which use the them interchangeably and others which distinguish them.'

Clearly this doesn't help if a definitive answer is what you want. It simply means what it says, that for years some groups of professionals have been saying that counselling and psychotherapy are the same whilst other groups of professionals have been saying they're different.

Do you think there are any differences between counselling and psychotherapy? What general impression do you get from media, publicity, friends, family and personal experience? Maybe you think you are not qualified to answer?

In his paper Brian Thorne looks at possible grounds for distinction including:

• The type of problem: psychotherapy is for deeper-seated problems.
• The type of treatment: psychotherapy uses the dynamics of the relationship between therapist and client.
• Duration of treatment: psychotherapy lasts for a longer time than counselling.
• The setting: psychotherapy takes place in medical settings, counselling in educational settings.

He concludes that there are no grounds for maintaining any difference in usage of the terms counselling and psychotherapy. He emphasises the need to clear up any confusion for the sake of our clients (in my terms for public relations purposes). Counselling, psychotherapy, call it what you like has a valuable contribution to make to our quality of life in the 1990s and confusion over names and titles will only serve to keep valuable skills away from those they are most likely to benefit.

Basic Helping

I have coined the phrase 'helping in a counselling way' to describe the type of *informed helping* we might aspire to on completion of a 20 - 30 hour introduction to counselling course.

This basic helping will incorporate an awareness of helping and counselling skills, but not the ability to offer a good range of them. In addition, this basic helping includes an awareness of the goals of counselling and the ethical framework within which professional counsellors work. Finally, we will be aware of the central role of self-development in the effective and responsible training of counsellors, together with the requirement for adequate support and supervision.

As a result of this new and developing awareness our ability as a helper at the most basic level will be improved. We will also be able to confidently assure ourselves, our relatives, friends, colleagues and others that we may try to help, that counselling is a responsible, skilled and useful helping activity whenever they might be in distress. This is basic helping. In Chapter 12 we will briefly review the learning on your basic introductory course and see where you might want to go next in the development of your helping skills.

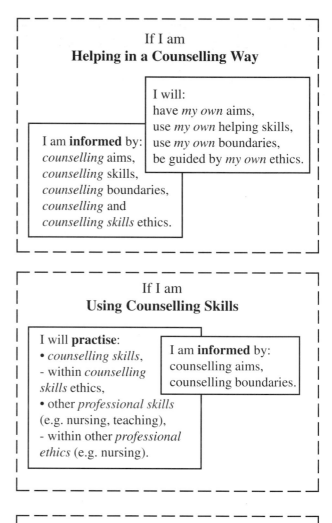

If I am
Helping in a Counselling Way

I am **informed** by:
counselling aims,
counselling skills,
counselling boundaries,
counselling and
counselling skills ethics.

I will:
have *my own* aims,
use *my own* helping skills,
use *my own* boundaries,
be guided by *my own* ethics.

If I am
Using Counselling Skills

I will **practise**:
• *counselling skills*,
- within *counselling skills* ethics,
• other *professional skills* (e.g. nursing, teaching),
- within other *professional ethics* (e.g. nursing).

I am **informed** by:
counselling aims,
counselling boundaries.

If I am
a Counsellor

• I will **practice** *counselling* skills.
• I will **keep** *counselling* boundaries.
• I will **have** *counselling* aims and goals.
• I am **governed by** *counselling* ethics.

Where Do Ideas in Counselling Come From? 2

There is much debate amongst counsellor trainers regarding the blend of ingredients in training. Just how much skills, theory and so on make the perfect training course? On a basic introductory course, the debate is whether to have theory at all. My view is expressed in this chapter, the title of which should give the game away; it's a thinly disguised '*Counselling Theory*' chapter.

When I first started helping as a volunteer at 'Off the Record' in Newcastle-upon-Tyne the training consisted of around three months of weekly meetings in which we discussed ourselves and did some role plays of 'problem' situations. At no time did anyone mention 'theory' or *where ideas in counselling come from*. Of course, it may have been assumed that, as a psychology undergraduate, I knew it all anyway. (This was not true, since my psychology degree didn't even have a section on 'personality'.) When I asked one of the trainers for more information, it was suggested that I read 'On Becoming a Person' by Carl Rogers. (I misheard the title and spent several hours approaching puzzled bookshop assistants asking if they knew 'I Am Becoming a Person'.)

Later I was thrilled to discover that someone had been thinking about helping skills in such a systematic yet approachable way. Then I discovered that Carl Rogers wasn't the only person to have thought deeply about human psychological distress. Indeed there were several approaches, theories and systems. Each one making claims to be successful and a new one seemed to be added to the list every week!

I decided to try to unravel this tangle of ideas, claims and counter claims. I discovered that the roots of the ideas can be traced as far back as you have the resources and energy to go. From centuries-old ancient philosophies and cultures through to current ideas in our own white European culture. A summary of the more recent landmarks goes back around 100 years ago to the work of Sigmund Freud. But first I want to look at some of the popular ideas we share about helping today, starting with the language we use.

'Like most psychologists, I appreciate the breath of fresh air which Freud introduced into the musty dry-as-dust atmosphere of nineteenth-century academic psychology. The brilliance of his mind has opened doors which no one now would wish to close again, and his keen insight has given us a storehouse of theories and hypotheses which will keep researchers busy for years to come.'

H.J.Eysenck: *Uses and Abuses of Psychology* p.241.

Imagine you are in the hypothetical situation of helping someone whose father has just died suddenly. Look down the following list of words. They are all ones we may associate with counselling, listening to and helping this person. Which ones are most likely to come to mind when you think about helping?

- Empathy
- Behaviour
- Manipulative
- Defences
- Positive Thinking
- Active Listening
- Genuine
- Goals
- Hidden Meaning
- Non-directive
- Client-Centred
- Dreams
- Unconscious
- Irrational Beliefs
- Making Plans
- Step-by-step
- Non-interpretative
- Avoidance
- Symbols
- Non-judgemental

All of these words can be traced back to three fundamental and very influential approaches to the psychology of human mental distress. We have assimilated many of the ideas which had their beginnings in these approaches into our modern culture and we make assumptions about effective helping which are directly attributable to these approaches to human psychology. Each approach has its founders and many more recent approaches to helping have been directly or indirectly influenced by these three schools of thought.

The founders of the approaches didn't invent these ideas out of thin air. Each is a product of a person in a social context at a moment in history. Each had their own influences from which they borrowed, sometimes acknowledged, sometimes not. The real picture of where ideas come from is, of course, much more complicated than this. It is probably impossible to fully understand the origin of ideas, but fun to try.

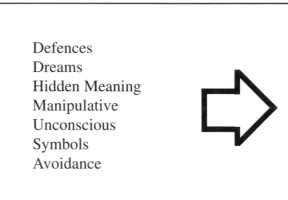

Defences
Dreams
Hidden Meaning
Manipulative
Unconscious
Symbols
Avoidance

Active Listening
Non-directive
Non-judgemental
Empathy
Genuine
Client-Centred
Non-interpretative

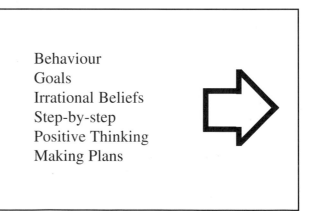

Behaviour
Goals
Irrational Beliefs
Step-by-step
Positive Thinking
Making Plans

Psychodynamic Approaches

Several contemporary approaches can all be traced back to the original work of Sigmund Freud, (1856-1939) founder of

Psychoanalysis

No contemporary psychologist or psychotherapist could claim not to be influenced by the work of Freud. Many schools of therapy grew more directly out of his work, sometimes founded by Freud's ex-students or associates, including C.G. Jung, Wilhelm Reich, Melanie Klien, D.W. Winnicott.

Modern counselling approaches influenced by Freud include Transactional Analysis developed by Eric Berne and Gestalt Therapy, developed by Fritz Perls.

Humanistic Approaches

Approaches developed by a group of American psychologists in the 1950s. In counselling terms, the most influential was Carl Rogers, (1902-1987) founder of the

Person-Centred Approach

Other influential humanistic psychologists, contemporaries of Rogers, include Abraham Maslow and Rollo May. Rogers ideas have had a wide influence in counselling, e.g. Gerard Egan incorporated Rogers' ideas into his highly successful systematic eclectic approach popularised by his book *The Skilled Helper,* (1975).

Many modern approaches to helping and education now claim to be person or student 'centred'.

Behavioural Approaches

Modern psychological approaches based on scientific learning theories of Russian Psychologist I.P.Pavlov (1849 -1946) and American psychologists J.B.Watson (1878-1958) and B.F.Skinner , founders of

Behaviourism

Skinner (more so than Watson) is another highly influential psychologist whose work has touched many modern ideas. 'Behaviour Therapy' became popular in the 1970s after Wolpe refined the work of the early Behaviourists.

Elements of learning theories can be found in most modern counselling approaches since all psychologists would acknowledge the role of learning processes of some sort in human development.

Why is theory important at this stage?

Helping is a skilled and responsible activity. Anyone wanting to improve their helping capacity needs to look at three aspects which contribute to their final performance as a helper:

• Theories •
• Skills •
• The personality of the helper •

A quick look at the contents page will reveal that each of these three aspects is represented in this book.

You may have thought that you know nothing about the theoretical origins of counselling before you started reading this chapter. I hope that pages 13 to 15 have shown that theory is not always something we get from books. Theories about how and why humans behave as we do are all around us in our culture. From the small, micro culture of our family and its myths to the large, macro culture of white anglo-America we get ideas about the way humans are. As I suggested before, ideas don't come out of thin air. Freud, Rogers, Skinner and others were all influenced by their respective cultures.

If I was to answer the question in the chapter title as briefly as possible, I would say 'Ideas in counselling come firstly from our own personal theories and secondly from books on counselling.' The aim of this section is twofold. Firstly to help you think about your personal ideas about human behaviour. Secondly to help you identify the possible origins of these ideas. You can then find and understand your starting point on theory in terms of ideas in contemporary psychology.

I am fascinated by theories, who thought them up and the circumstances under which they came to think them up. Add to that my belief that helpers should always be ready to explain what they are doing in terms a little more elegant than 'Just listening', 'Being caring' or 'Letting the client let off steam', and you will understand why I've included this chapter in an introductory book. I like to know a little about the main players in the theoretical field, so I've included some short biographical sketches of Freud, Rogers and Skinner on pages 26-28.

I will start by introducing a framework with which we will evaluate ideas. It has a superficial appearance of complexity, but I hope you will find it entertaining. On the next page you will find a series of scales on which we might have opinions about human personality and behaviour. Do you think, for example that we learn to be 'who we are' or that our personality is largely inborn, the result of hereditary factors? Do you think that we have conscious free will and can make emancipated decisions about how we act, or is our behaviour determined by unconscious motives beyond our knowledge and control?

If you go through the scales noting your position on each, we will move on to looking at how each of the major approaches fares on the scales. Then we will be able to find out where we fundamentally agree and disagree with each approach. It is common for people to find that their personal views are reflected by a mixture of ideas from each approach.

The idea for these scales comes from Hjeller, L.A. and Ziegler, D.J. *Personality Theories - Basic Assumptions, Research and Applications.* McGraw-Hill.

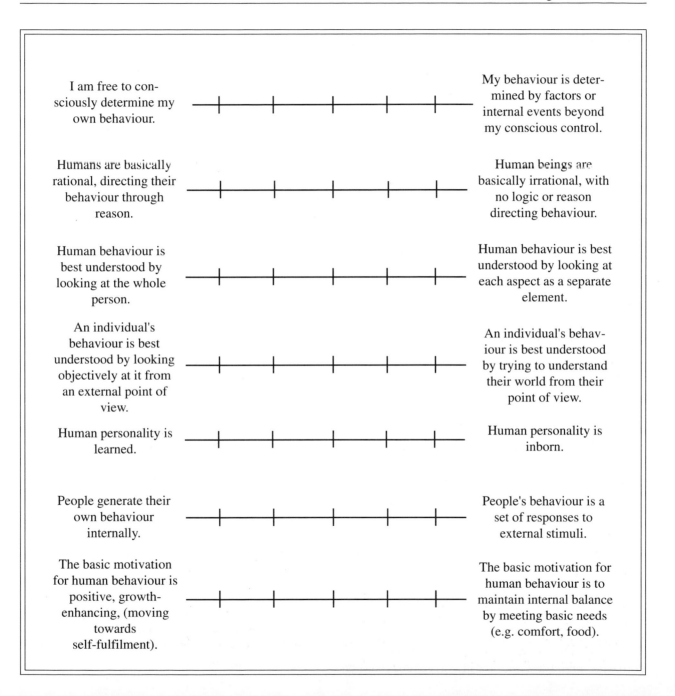

I am free to consciously determine my own behaviour.

My behaviour is determined by factors or internal events beyond my conscious control.

Humans are basically rational, directing their behaviour through reason.

Human beings are basically irrational, with no logic or reason directing behaviour.

Human behaviour is best understood by looking at the whole person.

Human behaviour is best understood by looking at each aspect as a separate element.

An individual's behaviour is best understood by looking objectively at it from an external point of view.

An individual's behaviour is best understood by trying to understand their world from their point of view.

Human personality is learned.

Human personality is inborn.

People generate their own behaviour internally.

People's behaviour is a set of responses to external stimuli.

The basic motivation for human behaviour is positive, growth-enhancing, (moving towards self-fulfilment).

The basic motivation for human behaviour is to maintain internal balance by meeting basic needs (e.g. comfort, food).

Psychoanalysis (Freud)

The Nature of Mental Activity

Freud believed mental activity existed in three domains:

- *Unconscious* or beyond our awareness and inaccessible. An individual can not gain access to her unconscious because it always remains hidden from her conscious mind. Hidden and inaccessible though it is, unconscious mental activity motivates much of our daily actions. The unconscious makes itself known through symbols, for example in dreams, which our conscious mind needs help in interpreting. Only through the process of psychoanalysis can this be revealed. The mental processes in the unconscious domain are chaotic and bizarre, obeying no laws of logic.

- *Pre-conscious* activities are those which although unconscious can be drawn into awareness through memory. Anything out of our immediate awareness which can be recalled, such as telephone numbers, postcodes, names etc., are pre-conscious.

- *Conscious* mental activity, fairly obviously, is the domain of full awareness. All thoughts and feelings of which I am aware are conscious. The conscious domain is governed by logical processes obeying the laws of reason.

Freud believed that everything we do and think has a 'goal'. There is no such thing as an accident or chance event. This is where the phrase 'Freudian Slips' comes from - indicating that our slips of the tongue are by no means accidental.

Structure of Personality

Freud divided human personality divided into three areas:

- *Id* This is part of the personality that we are born with. Freud described the id as a seething cauldron of instincts and desires which seek gratification at all costs. Id processes are unconscious, therefore chaotic and are ultimately pleasure and comfort-seeking. The id has no values, morals or concept of right and wrong. Its workings are most clearly seen in the behaviour of a new born baby. Freud called the inborn energy of the id the life energy or *libido* and he believed that it was largely sexual in nature.

- *Super-ego* This is the conscience, the internalised parent part of the personality. Freud believed that the super-ego formed when the child identifies with the same-sex parent, changing 'You must not do this' to 'I mustn't do this' so internalising rules, regulations, morals, notions of right and wrong, sex roles, etc. The development of the super-ego is basically a learning process. The strength of the super-ego is accounted for by the fact that it develops at a very early age (around five years old) when young children are very vulnerable and impressionable.

- *Ego* The ego develops through childhood, first as a mediator between the chaotic id and the outside world. The ego works out the consequences of behaviour aimed at satisfying the id and checks the id impulses based on reality. Later the ego has to appease the demands of the super-ego, so its task becomes a delicate balancing act. The ego is only fully developed at maturity. A properly adjusted adult is governed by the ego, balancing the 'I want it now!' demands of the id against the 'You mustn't do this you naughty boy!' admonishments of the super-ego.

The ego maintains control by using defence mechanisms which are unconscious. They help protect us from the demands of the id, often by simply avoiding the issue.

Psychoanalysis (Freud)

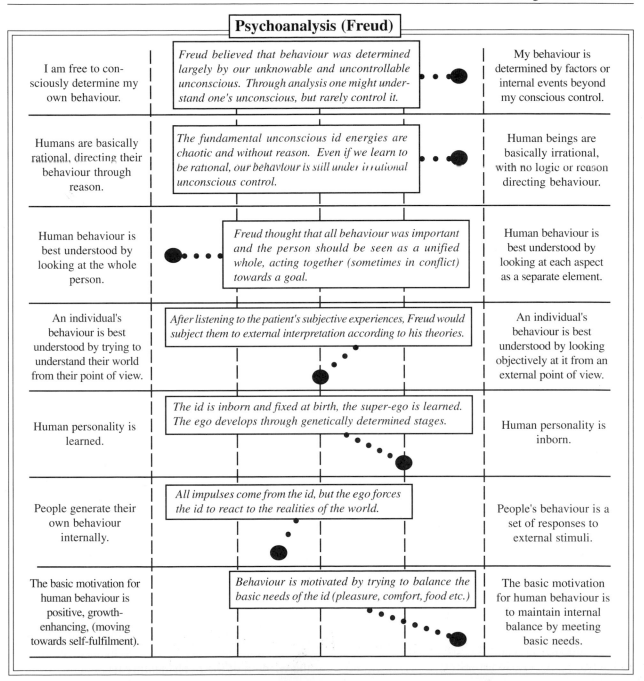

| I am free to consciously determine my own behaviour. | *Freud believed that behaviour was determined largely by our unknowable and uncontrollable unconscious. Through analysis one might understand one's unconscious, but rarely control it.* | My behaviour is determined by factors or internal events beyond my conscious control. |

| Humans are basically rational, directing their behaviour through reason. | *The fundamental unconscious id energies are chaotic and without reason. Even if we learn to be rational, our behaviour is still under irrational unconscious control.* | Human beings are basically irrational, with no logic or reason directing behaviour. |

| Human behaviour is best understood by looking at the whole person. | *Freud thought that all behaviour was important and the person should be seen as a unified whole, acting together (sometimes in conflict) towards a goal.* | Human behaviour is best understood by looking at each aspect as a separate element. |

| An individual's behaviour is best understood by trying to understand their world from their point of view. | *After listening to the patient's subjective experiences, Freud would subject them to external interpretation according to his theories.* | An individual's behaviour is best understood by looking objectively at it from an external point of view. |

| Human personality is learned. | *The id is inborn and fixed at birth, the super-ego is learned. The ego develops through genetically determined stages.* | Human personality is inborn. |

| People generate their own behaviour internally. | *All impulses come from the id, but the ego forces the id to react to the realities of the world.* | People's behaviour is a set of responses to external stimuli. |

| The basic motivation for human behaviour is positive, growth-enhancing, (moving towards self-fulfilment). | *Behaviour is motivated by trying to balance the basic needs of the id (pleasure, comfort, food etc.)* | The basic motivation for human behaviour is to maintain internal balance by meeting basic needs. |

Humanistic Approaches (Maslow & Rogers)

The views developed by several American psychologists (Maslow, Rogers, May) in the 1950s constitute what has become known as *humanistic psychology*. Whilst there are some differences between their ideas, there is an overwhelming convergence around some key themes. Rogers is best known for his theories as they relate to the practice of counselling and psychotherapy, and it is his ideas I will use as the basis for evaluation on the framework opposite. However, in order to build up a well-rounded picture, I will begin with some of Maslow's ideas.

Humanistic theories of personality maintain that humans are motivated by the uniquely human need to expand their frontiers and to realise as much of their potential as possible. These theories emphasise 'growth motives' and so contrast with both psychoanalytical and behavioural approaches which place their emphasis on reduction of biological needs.

According to **Maslow**, the motive to develop one's basic potential can take precedence over other motives including, occasionally, those related to biological needs. Maslow called this striving to achieve personal potential 'self actualisation'. He saw it as a pyramid of needs with the needs at each level having to be met before the next level can be approached meaningfully. We are always striving for self-improvement according to Maslow, and this goes beyond the simple meeting of our basic needs.

Carl Rogers' work concerning the process of change in therapy and education is based on the following fundamental propositions:

• That the fundamental underpinning or 'core' of human personality is constructive and good.

• That humans have this instinctive movement towards achieving their full potential in a constructive way, which he calls being 'fully functioning'.

• That this movement towards fulfilling one's potential includes an element of psychological self-healing.

• That the counsellor must provide the right conditions in which this self-fulfilling, self-healing process can flourish.

• That the right conditions are primarily when there is a complete absence of threat to the individual.

• That there is no single objective reality, just a collection of subjective ones.

• That the best vantage point from which to understand another person's behaviour is from their subjective viewpoint.

It is easy to see why Carl Rogers called his approach *Person-Centred*, since the client is the centre of the helping process in the sense that helping is seen as activating the self-healing process located in the client themselves by providing basic or *'core'* helping *conditions*. It is a respectful, non-threatening method, letting the client direct the process themselves through the wisdom of their self-healing tendencies.

5	**Self-actualisation**: the need to realise one's potential.
4	**Self-respect and esteem**: the need for status & self-confidence.
3	**Social needs**: the need for friendship and acceptance by peers.
2	**Safety needs**: protection from danger and need for security.
1	**Physiological needs**: need for survival, food, water, shelter.

Rogers (Person-Centred)

I am free to consciously determine my own behaviour.	*Rogers believed that behaviour is determined by conscious processes that are controllable and in awareness. There are no unknowable causes of behaviour.*	My behaviour is determined by factors or internal events beyond my conscious control.
Humans are basically rational, directing their behaviour through reason.	*The fundamental self is neither rational nor irrational in a superficial sense, but has a deep wisdom based on an underlying rationality.*	Human beings are basically irrational, with no logic or reason directing behaviour.
Human behaviour is best understood by looking at the whole person.	*Rogers believed that humans acted as organised, integrated whole organisms.*	Human behaviour is best understood by looking at each aspect as a separate element.
An individual's behaviour is best understood by trying to understand their world from their point of view.	*One of Rogers' fundamental propositions is that the best vantage point from which to understand someone's behaviour is from their point of view.*	An individual's behaviour is best understood by looking objectively at it from an external point of view.
Human personality is learned.	*The fundamental self, with the positive, growing tendency of the human organism is inborn. Almost everything else is learned.*	Human personality is inborn.
People generate their own behaviour internally.	*Impulses come from the self, and are acted upon. The organism reacts to a limited extent to the external world.*	People's behaviour is a set of responses to external stimuli.
The basic motivation for human behaviour is positive, growth-enhancing, (moving towards self-fulfilment).	*A fundamental humanistic proposition is that behaviour is motivated by the tendency to seek self-fulfilment. Even if human needs are arranged in an ascending order, the energy moves us to ascend to the highest level,*	The basic motivation for human behaviour is to maintain internal balance by meeting basic needs.

Behavioural Approaches (Skinner)

Academic psychology has made a patchy contribution to theories of helping and counselling. What often happens is that psychotherapists and counsellors call upon the findings of academic psychology to support their ideas, usually integrating several diverse findings to form a coherent therapeutic approach.

Much of modern psychology owes a great deal, at least in part, to the work of early behaviourists. Behaviourism grew in the early 1900s to all but dominate American psychology in the middle of the century. J.B.Watson and B.F.Skinner working separately and on different learning processes founded the movement which Skinner hoped would set humans free from the shackles of their existence by developing a technology of change and making it available to everyone. Armed with an understanding of learning processes, humankind would take control of their destiny.

The basic principles of behaviourism are:
- Apparently complex behaviour is a collection of more simple elements which can be understood in terms of basic learning principles.
- Learning or the acquisition of new responses, requires reward. (Punishment suppresses the expression of responses but doesn't eliminate them.)
- Human personality is acquired entirely through learning, i.e. human personality is a collection of favourite or most used responses based on those that have been most successful in the past.
- Behaviour is a set of responses where internal stimuli such as hunger, thirst etc. are paired with external stimuli such as the sight of food, drink etc.

in variously complex ways. Behaviour is therefore seen as being directed towards a specific goal.
- Whatever has been learned can be unlearned and modified through the application of learning principles.

These rather harsh and uncompromising views of the early behaviourists have been tempered in recent years by the incorporation of more 'human' factors such as thinking processes (e.g. positive thinking), attitudes etc. The nature of the learning processes themselves has been broadened to include more 'soft' processes such as learning by observation and learning without obvious physiological reinforcement (i.e. getting food or drink as a 'reward').

Some of these basic principles were marshalled into therapeutic methods by therapists such as Wolpe who refined a step-by-step method of overcoming irrational fears (phobias) by presenting people with more and more fear-provoking stimuli whilst they were relaxed. Similar efforts led to systems of reward where tokens were given to (for example) patients in mental hospitals for 'good' behaviour (perhaps related to their individual treatment plan) which they could exchange for privileges such as tobacco.

Behavioural approaches identify a clear goal which is achieved by repeated rewarded practice, often in small steps leading to the desired change. They are built on the idea that human difficulties and distress can be overcome by unlearning unproductive ways of thinking, feeling and behaving, then learning better, more fulfilling ways of behaving, thinking and feeling.

Behavioural Approaches (Skinner)

I am free to consciously determine my own behaviour.	*Skinner believed that behaviour is determined by stimulus-response associations beyond our control. Humans respond in a largely mechanistic way.*	My behaviour is determined by factors or internal events beyond my conscious control.
Humans are basically rational, directing their behaviour through reason.	*Skinner placed no value on rationality as an explanation of human behaviour. The principles of behaviour apply equally to all animals, so **rationality is not applicable***	Human beings are basically irrational, with no logic or reason directing behaviour.
Human behaviour is best understood by looking at the whole person.	*Skinner attempted to understand human beings by breaking behaviour down into separate elements or behavioural building-blocks.*	Human behaviour is best understood by looking at each aspect as a separate element.
An individual's behaviour is best understood by trying to understand their world from their point of view.	*External, objective measures of behaviour were the backbone of behavioural science. There is now some small room for subjective experience.*	An individual's behaviour is best understood by looking objectively at it from an external point of view.
Human personality is learned.	*This isn't called a learning approach for nothing. The idea is that we are born as a blank slate upon which our experiences in life leave marks. Learning is the basis of all personality.*	Human personality is inborn.
People generate their own behaviour internally.	*Humans are seen as almost entirely reactive. Behaviour is a reaction to the stimuli in the environment. Recent approaches acknowledge that internal stimuli, including thoughts, might also be the cause of behaviour.*	People's behaviour is a set of responses to external stimuli.
The basic motivation for human behaviour is positive, growth-enhancing, (moving towards self-fulfilment).	*Learning takes place in response to a need, for comfort, food etc. Some recent theories acknowledge that some human needs might be quite sophisticated, e.g. need for approval.*	The basic motivation for human behaviour is to maintain internal balance by meeting basic needs.

Re-examine the three panels on page 14 to see whether the words listed there are linked to the three approaches to human behaviour. It is clear that the following words are attributable to psychodynamic approaches and the work of Freud.

Defences	Unconscious
Dreams	Symbols
Hidden Meaning	Avoidance
Manipulative	

Similarly, the following words are attributable to humanistic approaches and the work of Rogers.

Active Listening	Genuine
Non-directive	Client-Centred
Non-judgemental	Non-interpretative
Empathy	

Finally, the following words are attributable to behavioural approaches and the work of Skinner.

Behaviour	Step-by-step
Goals	Positive Thinking
Irrational Beliefs	Making Plans

The point of this chapter is to help identify the origin of ideas, not to give a comprehensive introduction to these theories. The ideas and language in our 1990s culture owes much to psychoanalysis, humanistic and behavioural psychology, so more particularly, does the vocabulary of helping.

Where do you and your ideas fit in?

You might like to make a note of your views.

As you proceed in training, your helping style will be a mixture of your own deeply held views and new theories that you learn along the way. Here are very brief summaries of each approach.

Psychodynamic Approaches

Inborn instincts are the foundations upon which childhood experiences build our personality.

Our true motives are unconscious and hidden from us because the instincts and urges are taboo.

Our unconscious only lets itself be known to us indirectly through symbolic events like dreams or behaviour.

Using their knowledge and skill, the therapist interprets our experiences and behaviour (e.g. dreams) to unveil our unconscious motives, giving us an opportunity to be free of these unconscious controls.

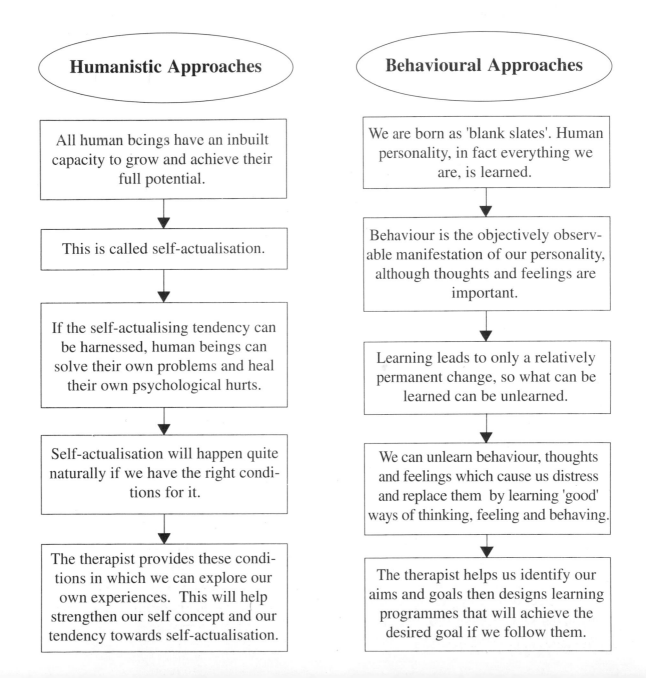

Humanistic Approaches

All human beings have an inbuilt capacity to grow and achieve their full potential.

This is called self-actualisation.

If the self-actualising tendency can be harnessed, human beings can solve their own problems and heal their own psychological hurts.

Self-actualisation will happen quite naturally if we have the right conditions for it.

The therapist provides these conditions in which we can explore our own experiences. This will help strengthen our self concept and our tendency towards self-actualisation.

Behavioural Approaches

We are born as 'blank slates'. Human personality, in fact everything we are, is learned.

Behaviour is the objectively observable manifestation of our personality, although thoughts and feelings are important.

Learning leads to only a relatively permanent change, so what can be learned can be unlearned.

We can unlearn behaviour, thoughts and feelings which cause us distress and replace them by learning 'good' ways of thinking, feeling and behaving.

The therapist helps us identify our aims and goals then designs learning programmes that will achieve the desired goal if we follow them.

Biographical sketches
(Psychologists are people too)

Sigmund Freud

Freud was born in Moravia, then part of the Austro-Hungarian Empire. When he was 4 years old, his family moved to Vienna where he lived until the last year of his life, 1939, which he spent in London having fled from the Nazis.

In 1837, Freud began his studies at the University of Vienna where his original interest was medicine and he conducted some importance research on the anatomy and physiology of the nervous system. In 1855 Freud went to Paris to study under Charcot who was experimenting with hypnosis in the treatment of hysteria. (Hysteria is when a person shows apparent physical symptoms such as blindness or paralysis without any physical cause. The condition also has the apparent purpose of gaining attention, e.g. hysterical paralysis of my writing arm before my exams!)

On returning to Vienna, Freud continued to use hypnosis in his treatment of patients during which time he learned that under hypnosis, people were able to 'reach down' below their ordinary consciousness and recall old, painful memories. Freud identified links between these memories with the present mental troubles his patients were experiencing.

From the case studies of his patients, dedicated self-analysis over a period of 50 years (he set apart half an hour at the end of each day for this), and discussions with his teachers and contemporaries, Freud developed his theories of psychoanalysis. His early theories place a strong emphasis on the role of sexual energy or drive in the development and structure of the personality. It would seem, for example, that during the informal discussion of a case Charcot suggested that the only thing that would surely benefit the patient was an active sex-life, of which she was deprived. Freud was deeply impressed by this and returned to Vienna with a deepening conviction regarding the role of sex in human psychology.

Whatever our views might be regarding the role of sex in our lives, it is clear that Freud's contribution to psychology has been incorporated into our culture. Many people accept that the unconscious mind exists and directs our behaviour hidden from view. We talk of Freudian slips, interpret each other's dreams and speculate about the 'real meaning' of a colleague's absence from work on the day his appraisal is due.

His work has attracted criticism since the late 60s from many quarters including feminists who contend that his basic ideas are anti-women. He believed that anything other than heterosexual penetrative sex was a 'deviation' from the natural, biological function of adult sex. It was a symptom of the sexual energy stuck in an infantile stage of development and therefore a suitable subject for treatment. Such views have been used for years to make the oppression of gays and women legitimate, by appearing to give academic or scientific credibility to prejudices.

Burrhus Frederick Skinner

Skinner was born in 1904 in Susquehenna, Pennsylvania into what has been described as a warm, stable family environment. In addition he notes that learning was esteemed, discipline prevailed (though never physical punishment), and rewards were given when deserved.

During his childhood, Skinner devoted much time and energy to building a variety of contraptions ranging from sledges and trolleys through to a device that would not allow him to leave his bedroom without hanging up his pyjamas! It has been suggested that this early fascination with mechanics was an indication of his later interest in modifying observable behaviour - also done in a somewhat mechanical way.

He majored in English at College and spent two years attempting to be a writer, during which time he found that he had little to write about. However, at the same time he became progressively more interested in psychology through the works of early behaviourists such as Watson. He went to Harvard University in 1928 to study Psychology.

In order to update himself on the emerging field of behavioural psychology he set himself a rigorous schedule of study involving an early rise, study before breakfast, his usual working day then study until bedtime with breaks of no more than fifteen minutes; a routine he maintained for two years

Like other innovators Skinner 'lived' his belief in behavioural principles, even using a controlled environment (referred to as a 'baby box') in the raising of his daughter. Similarities have been drawn between this device and the 'Skinner boxes' he developed to train rats and pigeons to press levers for food.

If Watson is seen as the 'father of behaviourism', then Skinner took the initial ideas and moulded them into a comprehensive scientific perspective. He has produced a large amount of published work and made a massive contribution to contemporary culture. Through his rudimentary attempts to help people with their problems using learning processes, he inspired *behaviour therapy* and indirectly the new very popular cognitive approaches.

His ideas have been particularly influential in education. His assertion that punishment does not help us get rid of unwanted behaviour, and the idea that learning should be a process of small steps to ensure almost continuous reward for inevitable success have given rise to changes in classrooms all over the world.

Carl Ransom Rogers.

Rogers was born in rural Illinois in 1902. A shy and quiet child, he went to the University of Wisconsin to study agriculture. Rather than pursue agriculture he decided to join the Christian ministry and went to Union Theological Seminary in New York City shortly after marrying his childhood friend Helen Elliot.

He soon took up the study of psychology at Teachers' College, Columbia University after becoming disillusioned with the more rigid doctrines of the church. He worked with children and their families for twelve years in Rochester, New York and during this time began to develop his ideas about the individual's capacity for self-help and the role of the counsellor as co-worker rather than expert in the helping process.

He continued to develop his theory through the 1950s after publishing Client Centred Therapy in 1951. Particularly concerned to validate his ideas through research, he made a huge contribution to research in psychotherapy throughout his life, inspiring thousands of projects in the 60s, 70s and 80s to evaluate the effectiveness of counselling and psychotherapy. Rogers himself undertook one of the largest studies into the use of psychotherapy with schizophrenic patients whilst at Wisconsin in the 60s.

He settled in La Jolla California where he founded the Center for Studies of the Person with like-minded colleagues. He continued to expand his breadth of vision beyond counselling and psychotherapy to relationships, education, politics and world peace. His particular contribution to contemporary culture was to put the individual, their experience and self-healing potential at the heart of the effective change process. This was a serious challenge to mainstream psychology at the time, which was busy trying to convince the world that psychologists were the 'experts' on human behaviour.

Rogers' views have been incorporated into our culture in many ways: not only do psychologists talk about being person or client-centred, but education now talks about being 'student-centred' and even industry and commerce want to be 'customer-centred'! Many in the 1980s and 90s are attracted to the basic humanity of his approach. One favourite criticism of his approach made by behaviourists is that the Person Centred Approach only works because when Rogers is understanding, genuine and warm towards his clients he is doing nothing more than teaching them to do the same and so they become understanding, genuine and warm themselves. If this is a criticism of the approach, I for one can't think of a better way to get things wrong!

Reshaping life! People who can say that have never understood a thing about life - they have never felt its breath, its heart - however much they have seen or done. They look on it as a lump of raw material which needs to be processed by them, to be ennobled by their touch. But life is never a material, a substance to be moulded. If you want to know, life is the principle of self-renewal, it is constantly renewing and remaking and changing and transfiguring itself, it is infinitely beyond your or my theories about it.

Boris Pasternak: Doctor Zhivago. p.282

The Importance of Self-Development

When planning this chapter, I considered calling it 'The Importance of Self-Awareness'. After all, self awareness is at the centre of developing as a counsellor. Then I realised that essential though self-awareness is, it's just not enough. It wouldn't be sufficient to sit back after a while with a satisfied smile and say, "That's it, I'm self-aware now!" The emphasis for counsellors is on a *process of improvement* not arriving at a given *state of awareness*. Knowing and understanding myself better is, however, the first step in this process.

In his book *Practical Counselling and Helping Skills*, (1993) Richard Nelson-Jones suggests that we could benefit from considering several areas of ourselves as a starting point for self awareness before we begin counselling, including our:

- Motives for helping.
- Capacity to feel.
- Sense of worth.
- Fears.
- Sexuality.
- Values and ethics.
- Culture and awareness of other cultures.
- Race and attitudes to race.
- Social class and attitudes to class.

The prospect of beginning a journey of self-exploration may seem daunting; many of us feel a strong urge to run a mile in the opposite direction

> 'All they had in them was themselves but they would keep going until they found what was in them to find.'
> Russell Hoban: *Turtle Diary*, p 170

> 'What may appear as coincidences are not coincidences at all but simply the working out of the pattern which you started with your own weaving.'
> Claude Bristol: *The Magic of Believing*.

whenever anyone mentions self-awareness. How do you feel about the prospect of looking at yourself, your motives, your fears, your sexuality, etc.?

Looking at the list of self-awareness topics opposite, how do you feel about exploring any or all of them?

•How would you go about the task of exploring or becoming more aware of, for example, your *capacity to feel* or your *sexuality*?

•Would you like to do this self exploration alone, in a pair with one other person, or in a small group.

•With friends, family or strangers?

Whenever we think about developing greater self awareness, we might have several feelings such as

Excitement
"Great I can't wait to get started!"

Fear
"Oh no, what dreadful things will I uncover?"

Relief
"At last, I've been meaning to do this for ages!"

What about you? Do you have any hopes or fears about self-development such as 'Leave well alone, all this thinking isn't good for you'. When you see this symbol:

✍ *MAKE A NOTE OF YOUR ANSWERS & EXAMPLES*

These feelings often come in conflicting bundles. It's difficult to shake off the notion that self-exploration is **risky**. We think we might get hurt or that, in some vague way, it might not be good for us. Better leave well alone, you never know what you might discover, and above all else don't do it with people around because it will make you vulnerable. I can clearly remember being told as an adolescent that I was too introspective and that I thought too much and too deeply for my own good!

Although we feel most at risk when we contemplate baring our soul to others, it is, paradoxically from the genuine responses of others that we stand to learn something about ourselves. By talking about ourselves as honestly as we can in a **safe** environment and listening to the feedback from others, we can check whether the view we have of ourselves is the

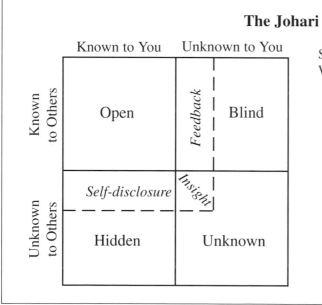

The Johari Window

Known to You   Unknown to You

Known to Others

Open | *Feedback* | Blind

Unknown to Others

Self-disclosure | *Insight*

Hidden   Unknown

Self-awareness can be 'mapped out' using a Johari Window:
- **Open** area is your open, conscious, public behaviour, known to you and others.
- **Blind** area is where others can see things about you that you cannot see yourself.
- **Hidden** area represents things we know about ourselves which we do not reveal to others.
- **Unknown** area includes feelings, thoughts and motives within you that are known to neither yourself nor others.

The open area is expanded by talking honestly about ourselves (*self disclosure*) and listening to *feedback from others*.

'It costs so much to be a full human being that there are very few who have the love and courage to pay the price. One has to abandon altogether the search for security and reach out to the risk of living with both arms. One has to embrace life like a lover.'

Morris West: *Shoes of The Fisherman.*

'And you may find yourself living in a shotgun shack
And you may find yourself in another part of the world
And you may find yourself behind the wheel of a large automobile
And you may find yourself in a beautiful house, with a beautiful wife
And you may ask yourself - Well...how did I get here?'

Once In A Lifetime: Talking Heads, words and Music by David Byrne, Chris Franz, Tina Weymouth, Jerry Harrison and Brian Eno.

one received by others. In addition we may discover some of the hidden motives that may have been influencing our attitudes and behaviour all along. This new self-awareness may make it possible for us to change, if we choose. This prospect of change may also bring new challenges.

It would seem, then, that the right environment is required before self-exploration feels safe. This process that we go through in training is similar to the process that a client might go through in counselling. We can now appreciate how vulnerable and frightened anyone seeking help might feel because we have experienced our own fears and joys on our own road to self-discovery. The conditions which lead us to feel safe enough to disclose some previously private feelings, are also similar to the conditions talked about by Carl Rogers (see Chapter 5), namely, empathy, non-judgemental warmth and genuineness or congruence.

High Challenge

Too scary, we get too frightened, defensive or hostile.	*The right balance for active participation in self-exploration. Exciting stuff!*
Low Support	High Support
Too dull, we become bored, disinterested and lose heart.	*Too comfortable and cosy, we don't get much work done.*

Low Challenge

In training, even on an introductory course, we need to be aware of an extra ingredient which will help us move towards greater self-awareness. That ingredient is the balance between feeling supported and feeling challenged. This balance point is different for everyone, and in a group we all share the responsibility for trying to get the balance right. If some of the issues in this book seem too low or too high in challenge, what can you do to increase the challenge for yourself, or increase the support you need to help you meet the challenge?

It is important to understand challenge. Too much challenge and we close down to learning, too little and we get bored.

Giving and Receiving Constructive and Effective Feedback

Giving and receiving feedback are two of the most important activities or processes in training in counselling and counselling skills. Feedback is both verbal communication (the words we say) and non-verbal communication (our actions, facial expressions and posture). It is through receiving feedback that we get an opportunity to see ourselves as others see us. It helps us become more aware of our behaviour - what we do and how we do it.

Giving Feedback
We can tell people how we see them.
We can tell people our feelings about the way they are.

Receiving Feedback
Others can tell us how they see us.
Other people can tell us their feelings about the way we are.

Both giving and receiving feedback can feel quite scary. What others think of us may not be in accord with our image of ourselves. This can be hurtful,

flattering or simply puzzling. Whichever it is, I find feedback either exciting or uncomfortable to give or receive - a little like playing the children's game of *'truth, dare, kiss or promise.'*

When others receive your feedback, they may also be feeling uncertain, uncomfortable or scared. Your impressions may well not fit in with *their* views of *themselves*. For these reasons, feedback needs to be thoughtful and given sensitively, not hastily, without thinking or like a 'bull in a china shop'.

You might be asked to give feedback to others on some personal issues on your course, such as whether you found the other person helpful, caring, sensitive and why. You may find the prospect of this daunting, but it requires no more than developing a sensitivity to other people's needs which is at the heart of good counselling. Here are some ground rules for giving feedback:

• All of your observations of another person will include both positive and negative elements. Try to include both positive and negative observations in your feedback. Avoid saying just negative things to the other person.

• What you are picking up is the behaviour of the other person. Comment on the other person's behaviour rather than give your impression of the person, i.e. 'Your voice had a very harsh quality.' rather than 'You are very harsh'.

• Stick to describing **what** you see or feel rather than either **making a judgement** about it or saying **why** it's happening, i.e. 'Your shouting frightened me.' rather than 'Shouting is a terrible thing to do, you do it because you are inadequate.'

• Try to give feedback on something that the other person can do something about, rather than something beyond their control.

• Speak for yourself not others, i.e. 'I think...' 'I feel...' rather than 'Everybody thinks...' or 'It's clear to everyone...' or 'I'm sure nobody knows...'

• Give feedback about specific instances or behaviours rather than generalising, i.e. 'When you did this.... I felt threatened.' rather than 'You threaten me'.

Personal Motives

Examining motives is a good thing to do whatever the activity in question. When considering involvement in counselling it is, at some stage, essential. It is crucial for us to be as sure as we can be, that our motives for offering to help someone will not distort the helping we can give so that it ends up being unhelpful or even damaging. Although we cannot hope to examine *all* motives here, we can look at a couple.

As an extreme example, there have been cases in the news recently where people working in children's homes have been found guilty of sexual abuse of the children in their care. It would seem that their motives for wanting to work with children were questionable.

Of course it would be stupid to suggest that we do not serve our own needs at some levels when we choose to volunteer or work as a helper. The question is, do our motives get in the way of our ability to offer constructive help, or do they facilitate our offering constructive help? Do these motives add to or take away from our helpfulness? For example:

• the central issue of *emotional pain* in my life can be the focus of helpful or harmful motives:

Helpful: If I have worked through a past traumatic event, I may have gained personal strength from the experience and also may be more sensitive to others suffering trauma.

Harmful: I may be over-sensitive to certain issues because my emotional pain is unresolved from a recent trauma. I might also be trying to resolve my own trauma through contact with clients, rather than trying to help the client.

• The central issue of *wanting to help others* can be the focus of helpful or harmful motives:

Helpful: Expressing an unselfish concern for others as helping behaviour can be seen as similar to the core condition of warmth or valuing others.

Harmful: If I require others to be dependent upon my help so that I can be seen as a 'good guy', I am distorting helping relationships to meet my own needs.

It is interesting to discover that there are certain safeguards that professional counsellors can make to guard against questionable motives and these are looked at in Chapters 7 and 8 on Ethics and Supervision respectively. Although a professional code of ethics and supervision of counselling practice are not strictly applicable to those interested in learning about a counselling way of helping on an introduction to counselling course, the principles of getting support for yourself and helping in an ethical way should be at the heart of everyone's helping activities.

'..it is his own hurt that gives the measure of his power to heal.'
Jung, C.G. *The Practice of Psychotherapy* par 239.

'The therapist is ultimately not there to treat the patient but, via a circuitous and well-concealed route, to treat or protect or comfort himself.'
Thomas Maeder, *Children of Psychiatrists and Other Psychotherapists.* p.77

'One would rather have a really suitable person for doing this kind of work than an ill person made less ill by the analysis that is part of the psychoanalytic training.'
Winnicott, D.W. *Therapeutic Consultations in Child Psychiatry.* p.1

Personal Values

Another of the many possible foci for personal development during a basic counselling course is the area of conflicting values. This might come up in four ways:

- Conflicts between different sets of values within myself.
- Conflicts between my values and my behaviour.
- Conflicts between my values and the values of the person I am in a helping relationship with.
- Conflicts between my values and the values of counselling (whatever I understand them to be).

As someone interested in helping others it is necessary for me to become aware of the values that I bring to the helping relationship since my own strongly held values may distort the help I am hoping to give. It is another tricky balancing act to try and offer genuine help in some areas of life without influencing a person's values by subtle means or maybe by disclosing my own values.

In terms of the core conditions discussed in Chapter 5, it is a matter of being simultaneously non-judgementally warm *and* genuine towards a person with whom you feel there is a conflict of values.

Similarly, if I have a conflict between two values or a conflict between my values and my behaviour, this incongruence will almost surely be picked up by the person I am trying to help, possibly making me seem ingenuine.

Examination of my personal values is therefore essential before I can be an effective helper.

Personal values, however, change as a result of life, new experiences, the passage of time...doing an Introduction to Counselling course. Although we might examine our personal values now, there's every chance that they might have changed by the time this book is finished. If I'm serious about being a helper, I must monitor my personal values to see how I change and develop. It might help to make a note now and look back at the end of this course to see if and/or how your values change.

✍

Counselling Values

Returning briefly to the three models of helping we overviewed in Chapter 2, you will realise that each one carries with it a set of attitudes about human beings and change. If we then look to the core conditions for effective helping proposed by Carl Rogers - empathy, non-judgemental warmth and genuineness - (see Chapter 5 for details), we find that the core conditions are more than just the foundations of good counselling and relationship skills. They suggest that in order to be effective helpers we need a certain set of attitudes and values as well.

Discussion Points on Personal Values: *How do you react to the following statements?*

Suicide and self-harm are wrong. If someone told me they were going to harm or kill themselves, I would do my utmost to stop them.

I could not listen to someone using sexist or racist language, I would tell them that it was wrong and to stop doing it. To listen without comment is to condone it.

I just couldn't sit in the same room as a child abuser. I would want to kill them!

I help people to make them happy. I would always try to end a session on a positive note.

I believe that there is nothing wrong with being gay, but I feel uncomfortable when gay people of my sex come too close to me.

I can't work out what my position on abortion is. I keep changing my mind. If I have an unwanted pregnancy, I suppose I'll work it out then.

For some of these issues, these are no 'right' or 'wrong' stands to take. Counsellors as a group, don't have a 'position' on suicide, or abortion. These are personal values regarding human life. However, there are some 'counselling values' which are generally held, e.g. counselling isn't about making people happy or cheering them up. Also, if you have conflicts between your values and your behaviour, then the process of personal development should help you resolve these before you start offering your help to others.

Discussion Points on Counselling Values:
How do you react to the following statements?

•People need help in understanding the hidden meanings in their life.

•People need to be offered a range of solutions to problems so that they can choose an appropriate one for themselves.

•People should have control over their own destiny.

•People have no right to make immoral or anti-social choices in counselling.

•We should take responsibility for the consequences of our actions, praise ourselves when we do good, admonish ourselves when we do bad, not praise or seek forgiveness from God.

•All people are equal and therefore are equally deserving of my help, regardless of who they are or what they have done.

These discussion points have been chosen to represent issues on which there is no 'party-line'. Counselling values may well conflict with your personal spiritual and political values. Will this conflict distort, or get in the way of, your helping capacity? Will being open to these conflicts through a commitment to personal development enhance your helping capacity?

These 'hidden' helping values may be:

• Completely new ideas to us.
• Familiar but different from the ones we are used to.
• Ones with which we totally and enthusiastically agree.
• Values with which we disagree in part or have difficulty in accepting.
• Attitudes with which we basically agree but have difficulty in genuinely displaying.

When we begin to explore helping we might have thought that counselling is value-free, or transparent to values or culture. After all, helping is just helping, isn't it? People wanting help is natural, and people offering help to each other is natural. The following are examples of possible values implicit in counselling processes:

• Change is a good thing.
• Change involves struggle and pain.
• People are basically good underneath the surface.
• Co-operation between equals is the best way to structure helping relationships.
• People are not born bad, they're made bad by the world and can therefore be helped to change.
• Some people are beyond helping.
• In order to be helped to change you've got to want to change.
• Counselling is for people with problems.

What do think the values implicit in *your* helping might be?

Feelings

That counselling is about, or involves the expression of, 'feelings' might seem obvious to many. Even though it's obvious, the prospect of *working* with feelings in some way, can *stimulate* many feelings in us. It's possibly the realisation that feelings beget feelings that makes some of us so anxious about looking too deeply at feelings. We might meet feelings or *emotions* in the following ways on a basic counselling course:

• *Listening* to someone talking about their feelings or emotions, i.e. they might tell us how angry they are.
• *Witnessing* someone express their feelings strongly, i.e. they might cry inconsolably in front of us.
• *Thinking* or *talking* about our own feelings or emotions, i.e. being reminded of how angry we were.
• *Expressing* our own feelings or emotions, i.e. feeling sad and crying on our own account, perhaps remembering some loss we have suffered.

Our general reaction to the expression of feelings and emotions will depend upon our values and beliefs about emotions. We will have acquired these values and beliefs from past personal experiences and from the views passed on to us from our upbringing and culture.

So, the famous British 'stiff upper lip' and 'passionate Latin temperament' are examples of ideas about cultural influences. Statements like 'she's got her mother's red hair, so she'll have her mother's fiery temper' might indicate family influences. Emotional expression is also linked to sex-role stereotyping. Women are supposed to be more open and free in expressing their feelings than men, who are supposed to 'keep it all in'. Like me, you might think that these

stereotypes are too rigid and simple to be applicable in everyday life. But then I ask myself why it is my wife who feels more able to cry than me when we go to watch a sad film?

Helping someone by listening accurately and sensitively to them means being sensitive to their whole person, including their feelings. I need to be able to respond to another person's whole range of expression, not have any blind spots caused by my own fear of expressing my own feelings.

What are your emotional blind spots? Are you afraid of feelings?

'I would say I'm sorry
If I thought that it would change your mind
But I know that this time
I've said too much
Been too unkind

I try to laugh about it
Cover it all up with lies
I try and laugh about it
Hiding the tears in my eyes
Cos boys don't cry'

Boys Don't Cry: The Cure. Words by Robert Smith.

'One way of putting this...is that if I can form a helping relationship to myself - if I can be sensitively aware of and acceptant toward my own feelings - then the likelihood is so great that I can form a helping relationship toward another.'

Carl Rogers: *On Becoming a Person*, p.51

Thinking and Understanding

There is so much emphasis put on feelings that some people believe helping in a counselling way is all about feelings and there is no room for thinking at all. Psychologists call our thought processes 'cognitions' and it is from this word that we get the title 'Cognitive Therapy'. There are a few approaches to change that put a high value on our thought processes by looking at how we keep ourselves unhappy by saying irrational things to ourselves such as:

• 'I'm unattractive, so no-one will ever love me and I will be unhappy for the rest of my life.'

• 'I daren't speak out in the group because everyone will see that I'm stupid and I will get so embarrassed that I'll blush and it would be the end of the world.'

Although we know that these thoughts are daft we have difficulty in trying to change them. We still behave as though they were true, for example, by never talking in a group. These patterns of thought can be really troublesome to many people and we need to be able to enter into their world of thoughts in order to understand.

The way I *understand* and *think* about my world is obviously important to me so when you are helping me I want you to see, accept and value my thoughts and understandings, not try to tell me that feelings are the only important bits of me. It is important to value your own thinking if you are to genuinely trust and value the thought processes of the person you are helping.

Personal Change

On the previous page we looked at counselling values and the possibility that change is a good thing. Whether or not you view change as a *good* thing, one thing is certain - counselling and helping is inextricably interwoven with personal change.

One way of thinking about change is to see it on a continuum, from big changes to small changes, and a continuum from high personal content to low personal content. Make a list of the changes that you have gone through in the past year. Then rate them in terms of whether they are big or small, and whether they involve a high or low personal content:

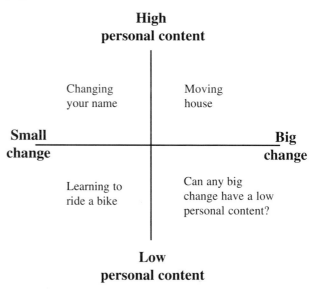

This grid will be different for each person, e.g. someone with restricted mobility, might put learning to ride a bike in a different place.

Psychologists researching the effects of change believe that change and coping with it is very stressful to human beings. I'm sure this will not come as news to anyone! However, you may be surprised to see the top 10 most stressful life events include moving house, divorce, bereavement and giving birth - consider whether they involve change, and where on our grid on page 38 they might fall.

Interestingly enough, psychologists also view learning as change because when we learn something new we have to re-arrange all of our previous knowledge to make room for (and make sense of) the new information. Learning that Father Christmas doesn't exist certainly made me review my experience in the light of new information. It was also very painful.

The idea that learning new things is painful is not a new one. Every time we learn something new we have to let go of an old view of things. What evidence is there in your life for these notions of change and learning?

Change is involved at many levels when thinking about helping in a counselling way:

- People ask for help because they want change: in simple terms they want to feel settled, happier and problem-free.

- People come to counselling because the want something to change: in simple terms they want to feel better. Or perhaps they are wanting to cope with an unwelcome change such as a bereavement.

- During training, even on an introductory course we want change: In simple terms we want to know more about helping in a counselling way and we might want to be better at it. Or perhaps we want to change some aspect of ourselves to become a better helper.

In order to cope with change we need support; both clients and those learning about counselling. Our personal reaction to change will affect the way we are able to help others cope with it. This is why, as people interested in helping, we must seek to understand our own thoughts, feelings and behaviour about change.

- If we are afraid of change or believe that change is a bad thing or have unhelpful ways of reacting to change in our own lives, we may distort the helping we offer clients, since change is often what they've come for.

> '...the more I am willing to be myself in all this complexity of life and the more I am willing to understand and accept the realities in myself and in the other person, the more change seems to have been stirred up. It is a very paradoxical thing - that to the degree that each one of us is willing to be himself, then he finds not only himself changing; but he finds that other people to whom he relates are also changing.'
> Carl Rogers: On *Becoming A Person* p.22

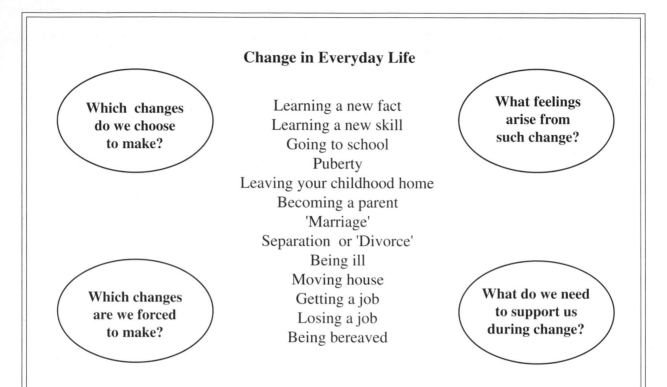

Change in Everyday Life

Which changes do we choose to make?

What feelings arise from such change?

Which changes are we forced to make?

What do we need to support us during change?

Learning a new fact
Learning a new skill
Going to school
Puberty
Leaving your childhood home
Becoming a parent
'Marriage'
Separation or 'Divorce'
Being ill
Moving house
Getting a job
Losing a job
Being bereaved

It is clear that change is common in our everyday lives and that it can be accompanied by strong feelings. These feelings can be negative or positive, however. Some ways of looking at change emphasise the transition from one state to another and suggest that our strong feelings are associated with the loss of the old (grief) and the shock of the new. It can be helpful to take a moment to consider change in your life and what it means to you.

In the Chinese language the same character stands for both 'crisis' and 'opportunity'.

Rather than see change as a threat, it is possible to see positive aspects in change. In business it is fashionable to look at the prospect of change in terms of *Strengths, Weaknesses, Opportunities and Threats.* By considering these elements of a change situation it is possible to see what can be gained from it.

'On our farm we have a row of maple trees that illustrate the mysterious process of adaption. Many years ago these trees were used as fence posts for the stringing of barbed wire around the pasture. Now, fifty or sixty years later, it is possible to look at those trees and observe the way the life process shows itself in adaptation. In some places the trees fought against the barbed wire as a hostile agent, and here the trees have long and ugly scars that deface the bark and inner structure of the trees. In other places, the barbed wire has been accepted and incorporated into the life of the tree. Where this happened, the barbed wire left no mark on the tree, and all that shows is the wire entering on one side and exiting at the other.

It is natural to wonder what makes the difference in the quality of a tree's response to injury. What was there in some trees that made them injure themselves by fighting against injury? What made it possible for other trees to be able to incorporate the injuring object and become master of the barbed wire rather than its victim?'

Edgar N. Jackson: *The Many Faces of Grief*, p.123-4.

'Can you find a wholeness that includes pain and a readiness to suffer?'

From The Religious Society of Friends: *Questions and Counsel*.

'Our futile effort at control impedes the flow we might otherwise have in our lives. Once we get out of our own way, we can become ourselves.'

Marilyn Ferguson: *The Aquarian Conspiracy*.

'Life is worth living. Not because there is nothing else, but because of what we each may give one another; pain, joy, anguish, peace. It's not an easy journey. You may even call it an adventure. It doesn't matter about the problems, the contradictions. In our hearts we understand everything. We understand it's the struggle that counts.'

Ann Oakley: *Taking it like a Woman,* p.204.

'Multiple and converging sources of evidence indicate that the person of the psychotherapist is inextricably intertwined with the outcome of psychotherapy. There is a dawning recognition...that the therapist him or herself is the focal process of change.'

Dryden, W. and Spurling, L. (Eds): *On Becoming a Psychotherapist*, p.215.

Keeping a Personal Journal

'Ever since I
Was a small child
I cannot sleep at night
With out the light on

I am afraid to laugh out loud
Or to stand out of the crowd
I am scared of loving you
I am afraid of losing you
I am afraid to lose control
I am afraid of growing old
I am afraid to die
But it's something I must do

It's not that I'm not strong
It's just that I'm not strong enough for you
It's not that I'm not brave
It's just that I'm not brave enough for two.'

I Am Afraid: A House, words by David Couse.

'if you ever get close to a human
and human behaviour
be ready to get confused

there's definitely no logic
to human behaviour
but yet so irresistible

there's no map
to human behaviour'

Human Behaviour: Bjork, words and music by
Gudmundsdottir, Hooper & Jobim.

Many courses, from basic introductions right up to diploma level and beyond, ask participants to keep personal journals to document their experiences during the life of the course in some way. Courses vary in their requirements, but most agree that keeping a personal journal can be a powerful aid in the process of personal development.

If your course does require you to keep a personal journal, you will receive any assistance necessary from the course tutors. If the process seems too vague for you, perhaps you could make that the subject of your first journal entry before asking the tutors for more guidance.

If you are not required to keep a personal journal, I would strongly suggest that you do. Both as a trainer and a participant, I have found personal journals to be useful, challenging, awkward, contentious and moving in equal measure. (Sometimes all at the same time!)

The next page is an extract from a personal journal kept by me when I attended a Person Centred Expressive Therapy Institute intensive twelve day residential course. I include it not as an example of good practice or model for journal-keeping, but to give an idea of what *I* have made out of journal-keeping. It *is* personal, and records some significant personal struggles of my own. (I wrote the original diagonally across the page.)

January 10th

Day 2 of the Expressive Therapy course and my second journal entry. Although I feel I am writing this mainly out of duty, I do feel quite been to see what happens as I set pen to paper. Should I give an account of today or just pick up on anything that has moved me? We started today with movement, as we will do each day, at 7.30am before breakfast. I have been re-acquainted with my board-like body. Boy was I stiff!! With my arthritis of recent years and my lack of exercise my movement has become very restricted. I think it may be a metaphor for my whole life, since I know I am capable of a wider range in play or... than I currently display.

Why is that? How can I loosen up in life?

I thought I would find the free movement stuff difficult. It has turned out to be easier and more enjoyable than my typically conservative expectations. Expressing myself freely by moving around is still difficult. In relationships, at work, in play or... for me. I feel stupid, exposed, vulnerable. Maybe people will laugh at me? The whole group movement directed by Shellee was brilliant. It has turned out to be easier Just very moving...nearly everyone was crying, me too...simple meeting...connecting...and all the things I can't, don't or won't do in everyday life. I think I was crying for myself and all of the lost opportunities to make connections with people like this. Natalie did a counselling demonstration today which was interesting and, I was impressed. She asked the group to take part at one point which I thought was great. I am constantly impressed by her genuineness ('in a technical sense) when she is feeling. She is facilitating the group or counselling an individual, She never lets an opportunity go by without letting us know what she is feeling. She does it in a way that doesn't intrude, direct or push. I must get a handle on it since I would like to be able to do it too. It's a very powerful tool....

January 11th 11pm.

I have real difficulty in understanding D sometimes. I can't get a handle on why - she seems so airy ('in the elemental sense of the word) so delicate, so 'other-worldly' that the contact we make is like the landing of a butterfly on my hardest, most insensitive skin. She and I seem to be from different planets. I think she senses this too, but I don't know for sure, and this is further testimony to our unconnectedness I shrink from raising the issue for fear of it exploding like a dandelion clock in a puff of wind. She is like a fragile fluttering bird and I fear that she could hurt me.

Prejudice, Oppression and Counselling

4

When we concentrate so much on the individual and their needs as we do in counselling, we can sometimes lose a certain perspective. That perspective is the one which gives us a glimpse of the real world and the forces active within it that affect us as individuals. The real world that I see is often harsh and brutal with many inequalities. I don't want to lose the harsh 'edge' to this view by wearing rose coloured spectacles.

Sometimes the world of counselling and helping can be a little like a pair of rose-coloured glasses, through which I see people making choices about their lives in the safety of a helping relationship. The truth is, of course that the real world gives me, a white, middle class, able-bodied, heterosexual man with a university education, many more opportunities and choices than anyone else. Can a counselling way of helping make any headway against prejudice and oppression?

We should always be aware of what helping in a counselling way can realistically achieve. There is a tendency for us to get too enthusiastic about the possibilities and very soon we start to believe that counselling can be a cure for everything.

On the other hand, some people think that counselling, with its concentration on the individual person, fails to take into account important social processes. Then, rather than being part of the cure, counselling is seen as the disease since a counselling way of helping can appear to say;

'Let's talk about why you are depressed - it'll get better if you share your troubles.'

However, talking won't get this person a job and decent housing or stop the racial abuse. It is important that helpers and counsellors do not turn away and walk on the other side of the street whenever prejudice and oppression raise their heads. If a counselling way of helping gives us the privilege of being let into, and understanding, another person's world, we should be prepared to face up to the unpleasant truth that sometimes we (yes, uncomfortably, me too) may be part of the problem.

My purpose in spending time considering prejudice and oppression in an introductory book is to acknowledge that the roots of prejudice and oppression are very deep and we simply cannot start too soon to understand our own attitudes and how we turn them into behaviour.

If we put such a premium on self-awareness then we must surely want to become aware of our prejudices and if we are so keen on self development, then we must surely try to live our lives in a way that doesn't oppress others.

Many books and courses concentrate on culture and race as the focus of their work on prejudice and oppression. In this book, I am simply going to set the process in motion by looking in more general terms at differences between people, e.g. differences in colour, class, gender, religion, culture, sexual orientation or whatever, and how we often translate those differences into prejudices.

Prejudice

Prejudice has been defined as: 'an attitude that predisposes a person to think, feel, perceive and act in favourable or unfavourable ways towards a group or its individual members' (Secord and Backman, 1974). This means that our views and beliefs will reveal themselves in the way we show preferential treatment towards, e.g. ourselves and 'our group' and when we try to disadvantage others and 'their group'.

If we wish to help in a counselling way, we must do something to become aware of our prejudices so that we can understand the way they will affect our helping relationships. We will see in Chapter 5 how important it is to be able to be respectful, warm and accepting towards the person you are trying to help, whilst also being genuine. This is clearly going to be difficult if you harbour prejudices towards people.

Most of us who are drawn towards helping others like to think that we are a prejudice-free zone. It might come as a surprise to learn that this is not the case. However open-minded we like to think we are, we will have prejudices directing our behaviour. As a white man, I can only think as a white man with all of the views, perspectives and prejudices of a white man.

In some circumstances we tend to focus on the similarities between people, the things that bind us together as humans. Under other circumstances we emphasise the differences. A counselling way of helping tries to capture the positive elements of both similarities and differences - whilst celebrating everyone's uniqueness and their individual qualities, we also want to respect their rights as a human being - to be treated as an equal, with dignity.

What comes into your mind when you think about the word prejudice?

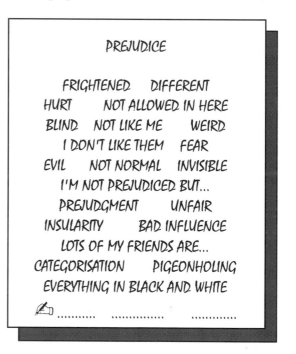

PREJUDICE

FRIGHTENED   DIFFERENT
HURT   NOT ALLOWED IN HERE
BLIND   NOT LIKE ME   WEIRD
    I DON'T LIKE THEM   FEAR
EVIL   NOT NORMAL   INVISIBLE
    I'M NOT PREJUDICED BUT...
    PREJUDGMENT   UNFAIR
INSULARITY   BAD INFLUENCE
    LOTS OF MY FRIENDS ARE...
CATEGORISATION   PIGEONHOLING
EVERYTHING IN BLACK AND WHITE
....

The flipchart above illustrates the views of our hypothetical group that we first met in Chapter 1. When you think about this hypothetical group, who do you picture; a mixed group of men, women, black, white, gay, straight? In your mind's eye, who is missing? Did your imaginary group have no black people, no men? What does your mental picture say about your prejudices?

Prejudice revolves around a negative view of difference - the differences between you and me. When you see this symbol:

✍ *MAKE A NOTE OF YOUR OPINIONS & EXAMPLES*

The sort of dimensions on which we judge these differences include:

Race/Ethnicity
Nationality
Religion
Class
Gender
Sexual orientation
Age
Dis/ability
✍ Any other dimensions you can think of.

What is it in your experience about these dimensions of difference that cause so much prejudice? What do you think?

✍

Let's look at a few statements to find out where we stand in relation to some of these issues. The questions are sometimes deliberately contentious to get us thinking about our prejudices. We may find that powerful feelings accompany our views on these issues. These feelings are signals that the issues are connected to deeply held views which may be difficult to confront and change. The process must start, however, with raising our awareness. When looking at these statements, try to stay with your first, gut reaction.

• Private clubs should have the right to exclude people on the grounds of gender, disability, race, colour or religion.

• If black people really wanted to get on in life, they would stay on at school and work harder.

• Women have made no real progress in getting equal treatment in recent years.

• All children should speak English at school.

• I would be very happy if my son or daughter told me they were gay.

• Other people's religious rituals are daft - fancy not eating milk and beef together, or not using a toilet that faces east!

• There's plenty of jobs if you go looking for them, the dole is just for scroungers who don't want to work.

• Everybody over the age of 55 should be made to retire to make more jobs for the younger people.

What are your reactions to these statements? Do you disagree and feel angry about them or agree passionately?

Power

A counselling way of helping is based on a recognition that all humans are equal. It may seem strange, therefore, to look at power in counselling relationships. It would be convenient to think that we are equal to all those we are trying to help but on one basic dimension, there is an inequality - they are asking us for help. There are certain factors which shift our sense of power in relation to others; some factors shift it up and some factors shift it down.

Being between the ages of 25 - 45
Being middle or upper class
Being white
Being English speaking
Being articulate
Being educated
Being a counsellor
Being employed
Being able-bodied
Being tall
Being 'attractive'
Being a man.

Factors which shift power up.

Being black
Being young
Being a woman
Being old
Being short
Being a client
Being uneducated
Being unemployed
Stuttering and stammering
Having a strong regional accent
Not speaking English well
Being a victim (of violence, abuse etc.)

Factors which shift power down.

Are there any other factors in your experience that have had the effect of giving you more power or less power?

People frequently ask me, "Are you Carl Rogers' daughter?" It has taken women's groups like these to raise my consciousness to give the appropriate answer to that question which is "Yes, I'm the daughter of Helen and Carl Rogers."

Natalie Rogers: *Emerging Woman*, p.170

Differences in power between counsellor and client may have a number of effects. We need to be aware of potential power and status differences in our helping relationships so that they do not get in the way of us offering help.

• Some people are uncomfortable about asking for help unless the helper is seen as equal, i.e. they want a companion or someone to help in a co-operative way.

• Some people are uncomfortable about asking for help unless the helper is more powerful or higher status, i.e. they want help from an expert whom they think will give them good quality help.

• As a helper do you think your helping is only effective if you and your client see each other as equals?

• Some women do not want to receive help from a man.

• Men from some cultures would not ask for help from a woman.

What specific examples of power differences can you come up with that might give rise to problems in helping relationships?

✍🗀

Oppression

This is one of those words that I think I *know* the meaning of, but I really don't *understand* it. As I mentioned before, I must be one of the least oppressed people around. I looked in the dictionary for a definition and read that oppression is 'prolonged cruel or unjust treatment or control.' Other words come to mind - what do you think of when the word 'oppression' is mentioned.

OPPRESSION

ABUSE   HARASS   DO DOWN
MISTREAT   SUPPRESS   DICTATOR
TORTURE   PAIN   TORMENT
PERSECUTE   DISCRIMINATE AGAINST
STOP US GETTING JOBS
GLASS CEILING   SEGREGATION
HARDSHIP   SLAVERY   OVERPOWER
APARTHEID   MEN OPPRESS WOMEN
SUBTLE   UNSPOKEN SECRET CODE
NO JOBS, NO HOUSING   GHETTO
INEQUALITY - EQUAL RIGHTS FOR ALL

✍🗀 ....

Above is a flipchart with the thoughts of our imaginary group. How did you get on - and how did you feel? Did you think that oppression has nothing to do with you? Perhaps like me you feel fortunate or in some way protected from oppression? This doesn't mean that we should or can do nothing.

I wish I could remember who it was that said 'If you're not part of the solution - you're part of the problem'. This phrase seems to catch the feeling exactly and asks me what *I* am doing about *my* attitudes and behaviour.

A good starting place is to understand yourself better in terms of what gives you your own identity and realise that this gives you certain viewpoints and perceptions. So to return for a moment to the list of 'power factors' on page 48, how do these factors contribute to your sense of identity - i.e. your race, colour, religion, physical stature, gender, education, class, physical ability and status, etc?

Asking such questions can be a painful process, so I would not recommend you get too deep without support. Perhaps you could try it with a friend or someone else on your introductory course.

As a white, middle class, able bodied male, I have a set of perceptions which are particular to that group. I cannot see into the worlds of disabled people, women or black people with ease, if at all. It is difficult or impossible for me to understand and insulting of me to claim to be able to, but I can *try*. If I am sensitive and humble in the trying, then I may be experienced as empathic.

'There are several natural reactions on the part of white Americans which are of no help whatsoever: 'I can understand your bitterness because I've been oppressed too'; 'Yes, yes, I can understand how you feel, but I have never personally been a part of your oppression. It is the white society which has oppressed you.' Whites who are effective seem to learn two attitudes - one toward self and one toward the minority members. The first is the realisation and ownership of the fact that 'I think white.' For men trying to deal with women's rage, it may be helpful for the man to recognise 'I think male.' In spite of all our efforts to seem unprejudiced, we actually carry within us many prejudices.'

Carl Rogers: On Personal Power. p.204.

After trying to understand your own position and prejudices better, it can help to try to give oppression some personal meaning:

• Think about a time when you have experienced oppression yourself. (You may have difficulty in admitting to being oppressed, but most people have been oppressed at some time in their lives; perhaps because of your nationality, religion, accent or during childhood.)

  • What were your thoughts and feelings at the time?

  • What did you want to do about it for yourself?

• Did your oppressors realise that they were oppressing you?

• What did you want the person or people responsible to do about it?

This last question is important since it seems reasonable to find out what an oppressed person wants from you that would help - and to listen very carefully. And secondly if all else fails, we could fall back on the old proverb: 'Do as you would be done by'.

Finally, let's not assume that because everyone may have experienced oppression at some time in their lives, this means that we can ignore the issue since it all somehow cancels out. There are many inequalities built into the system in this and most countries. These inequalities oppress both individuals and groups, restricting their freedom to live fulfilling lives. This institutional oppression is familiar to all of those with some of the negative factors listed on page 48. Systems are staffed by and voted for by individuals, so we all have a role in maintaining such institutional oppression. We could do well to ask ourselves whether we do anything to oppose oppression when we get the opportunity.

Language
One way in which the system oppresses people is in the way language is used to devalue people, to exclude and invalidate their experience. There has been a lot of publicity recently concerning PC or *Political Correctness* and the issue of language. My own view is that since as a counsellor I try to choose my words with care, I am careful to not contribute to the continuing oppression of others by using offensive or demeaning language.

The current jokey 'backlash' against so-called *Politically Correct* language just diverts attention away from the real issue. If we are to be respectful towards each other in helping relationships, this must surely include the language we use. Who in 1994 would say 'nigger' other than someone with racist intent? Our language is a window to the attitudes we hold, so first of all note the words you use, then wonder whether you might find them offensive if used to describe you.

What else can I do?
There are many subtle ways in which we are all racist, sexist, ageist, failing to see the value in other people because of their religion, class or whatever. One way is to think that there are no differences. If I say, "I'm not racist, I treat everyone the same!" I am failing to acknowledge the important *differences* between people which give each of us our identity. A useful phrase which sprung from the women's movement in the seventies was 'different but equal' meaning that women do not want to be seen as the same as men at all (and black people do not want to be seen as the same as white) but as different with valid, useful differences worth celebrating.

If we think that everyone is the same, it is racist and sexists since it denies the culture, religion, history and biology that makes us different. Does the organisation you work for reflect the community which it serves? How much effort do you personally put in to find out about different cultures?

As with so many things, actions speak louder than words, and if you get involved, you will learn about the issues through reading, meeting people and making friends.

• If you work for an organisation:

Familiarise yourself with the equal opportunities policy and help monitor the way it is implemented.
If there is no equal opportunities policy could you propose one and work with any oppressed groups to write it?

• What can you do to get to understand the issues better:

Have you got a list of contacts for local groups for women, gays, lesbians, different ethnic communities, disabled, etc.?
Have you made contact with any for literature, to meet with the staff, to discuss their services?
Have you sought out any specific training or personal development opportunity on race, sexuality, oppression, power?

• Make an effort to learn about different cultural and religious groups in your community:

Most agencies, hospital wards and colleges 'celebrate' Christmas. What message does this give to the users of your service?
Do you know when the religious festivals of other ethnic groups are?
Does your organisation celebrate them or even acknowledge that they exist?

• Oppression is a personal and a political issue.

> If you wish to be more active in understanding and counteracting oppression you will have to familiarise yourself with some of the political issues involved. This will take time and patience, since you may well find yourself excluded from some groups and sources of information because you will be understandably seen as one of the oppressing group. It is important to accept and work with this perception and requires some empathy, effort and willingness to change on your part.

None of these suggestions is going to change the world overnight, but they do give you some power in your own sphere of influence. The process of change in your sphere of influence starts with yourself and then stretches out to include your family, friends and colleagues.

It is our belief that, to some extent, all individuals are racist, sexist, and classist.

In a setting such as this, some of these will become explicit. It is our hope that everyone will be understanding, respecting, empathic and non-judgemental.

In a setting such as this we should all be allowed to make mistakes.

Joyce Thompson, 1985

Counselling and Helping Skills

Most people now look upon counselling as a skilled activity practised by trained people acting in a 'professional' way, i.e. according to a set of standards. It has not always been the case. Indeed when I first started as a volunteer counsellor in 1973 I spent a lot of time defending the skills of counselling (as I understood them then) from the assertions of others that counselling was variously: 'Just chatting.' 'Just listening.' or 'Just being someone's friend.' I seem to remember that such put-downs always had the double barb that firstly counselling is what people do anyway ('chatting, listening or being a friend') and secondly that it was 'just' or 'simply' that and nothing else. It was not something I had to learn, could benefit by practice at, or would get better at by receiving constructive feedback from others. In other words it was not a skill.

> **Skill** an aquired higher-order activity to perform complex... acts smoothly and precisely.
> *Longman Dictionary of Psychology and Psychiatry (1984)*

The idea that human beings use skills to manage relationships is not a new one. This view gained considerable popularity in the 1970's when the notion of social skills seemed to be cropping up everywhere. Social skills was the term used to indicate that the business of being a social being - having to live a life in the presence of others, in parallel to others and interwoven in the lives of others - was indeed a matter of skill. The idea that social skills were important in everyday life soon became accepted and since a skill can be learned and improved with practice, social skills training was set up to help develop the particular type of social skills necessary to have a good marriage, be a good salesperson, be an effective manager, etc.

The idea that helping in general ,and counselling or therapy in particular, could be looked at as a set of components which could be learned was made popular by Carl Rogers when he wrote about the 'core conditions'. (Mentioned briefly in Chapter 2.) Nowadays it is accepted that counselling is skilled and that practice makes better, if not perfect. Most training courses spend a lot of time getting trainees to practise their counselling skills. The question is:

What are Counselling Skills?

This question is closely related to the work covered in Chapter 1 'What is Counselling?' In the search for possible definitions of counselling we compared it to other helping roles we are familiar with. So to answer the question What are Counselling Skills? I would ask you to consider other helping roles alongside counselling, e.g. the same ones as in Chapter 1.

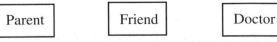

DOCTOR

GOOD AT EXPLAINING MEDICAL THINGS IN EVERYDAY LANGUAGE

ACTIVE LISTENING

KEEPING PROFESSIONAL DISTANCE

CREATE A SAFE ENVIRONMENT TO TALK ABOUT PRIVATE THINGS (CONFIDENTIAL)

✍ ....

FRIEND

OFFERS PROTECTION

COMPLETE DEPENDABILITY, HONESTY AND LOYALTY

GENUINE (NEVER CALLS YOU NAMES BEHIND YOUR BACK)

IS ON YOUR SIDE

ACTIVE LISTENING

✍ ....

PARENT

ACTIVE LISTENING

EVEN-HANDED AND FAIR WITH DISCIPLINE

SUPPORTIVE

GIVING UNCONDITIONAL LOVE (NON-JUDGEMENYAL)

UNSELFISH & GENEROUS

ABSOLUTE TRUSTWORTHYNESS

✍ ....

COUNSELLOR

ACTIVE LISTENING

BEING GENUINE

NON-JUDGEMENTAL

OFFERS CONFIDENTIALITY

EQUAL (ON THE SAME LEVEL AS YOU)

SUPPORTIVE

✍ ....

The flipcharts above show a selection of ideas about the kind of helping skills needed in different roles (similar to those we saw in chapter 1) and it is clear that some common helping skills are emerging. Are your ideas similar or very different? How much do you agree with the list of counselling skills on the flipchart? When you see this symbol:

✍ *MAKE A NOTE OF YOUR ANSWERS & EXAMPLES*

In Chapter 2, I looked at where the ideas behind modern counselling approaches have come from and it is useful to ask *ourselves* where *our* ideas have come from. What has influenced your ideas on counselling skills? Have your ideas about *counselling skills* come from:
- Personal experience of being counselled?
- The beliefs of friends and family?
- What you've read in the papers or seen on TV?
- Someone you know who is a counsellor?
- Books about counselling or psychology?
- Other books, e.g. novels or spiritual writings?

It is not realistic to expect to be properly trained in the use of counselling skills on a course lasting less than around 100 hours, but it is realistic to expect to raise your awareness to what counselling skills are and to have a go at trying them out to see how it feels. It is in this spirit that I offer the following sections:
- To help you identify the skills you already have.
- To back up any skills training you may be doing.
- To help you further develop your repertoire of counselling skills.
- To give some more detail on the skills you might be encouraged to practise.
- To show a range of skills which you may not otherwise be able to cover due to time constraints.

The Work of Carl Rogers and Gerard Egan.
In Chapter 2 I looked at the origins of theory in counselling, briefly touching upon the work of Carl Rogers and just mentioning the work of Gerard Egan.

My own practice has been influenced most heavily by the ideas of Carl Rogers, but I acknowledge the importance of the ideas of Egan in developing counselling practice, especially in the UK.

Both Rogers and Egan were responsible for developing the idea that counselling was a skilled process, and most would agree that Egan incorporates Rogers' ideas into his framework for understanding the process of helping. Most training courses now emphasise the development of skills as an important, indeed essential, element in training to be a counsellor. At an introductory level we must be content with the basic underlying principles.

You may remember from Chapter 2 that Carl Rogers developed his ideas in the 1950's, continuing to refine them until his death in 1987. He proposed that the helper or counsellor needs to provide the right conditions before the natural, positive, self-healing tendency within the client is activated or enhanced. Rogers suggested that the 'right' conditions involved the complete absence of threat to the client. He went on to elaborate his ideas in 1957 and proposed that the central conditions in a helping relationship were:

- Empathy
- Congruence or *Genuineness*
- Unconditional Positive Regard or *Non-Judgemental Warmth* or *Acceptance*

These 'core conditions' proposed by Rogers form the basis for many skills-approaches to counselling, even though Rogers himself was keen to emphasise the important role of the relationship in the helping process. He did not see counselling as just assembling a set of skills; rather he believed that counsellors must incorporate the core conditions into their ways of being as people.

Becoming a counsellor does indeed involve a deal of personal change for the counsellor-in-training, but at this stage we will simple identify some basic counselling skills that emerge from the core conditions. Firstly a closer look at the core conditions themselves.

Empathy
This is trying to see the world of another person from their point of view. It involves trying to understand their world, their meanings, their life. It has been described as walking in someone else's shoes, understanding how they feel and think - listening to both the 'words' and the 'music'. The emphasis is on not only understanding, but also on doing this gently and sensitively, then communicating this to the other person. Not trampling around their world of personal images and meanings without any care.

Being empathic is:

1. Listening sensitively.

2. Trying to make sense of what you hear.

3. Understanding the other person in their own terms.

4. Checking to see if you've got the meaning right with all its subtleties.

Carl Rogers describes empathy as the ability to sense the client's world *as if* it were your own, without losing the 'as if' quality. He placed particular emphasis on being able accurately and sensitively to understand the client's *feelings* without getting them muddled up with your own. He makes it clear that we cannot actually put ourselves into the world of others, we can never experience the same things as others. Even if we have a similar experience, we will not have felt exactly the same about it.

A good example is bereavement. I can remember when my dad died quite clearly. I was 18 years old and it was three weeks before my A-level exams. I was sure that the pain and loss I felt could not be experienced by anyone else, not even my brother. I knew that his relationship with Dad had been very different from mine (he was 14 at the time). The experience of the loss of a parent, close relative or friend is different for everyone. Some people may feel relief or a sense of freedom if their relationship with their parent was restrictive or burdensome. Such responses can be very difficult to cope with if they come along with a sense of pain and grief at the loss.

It might be tempting to think 'Ah yes, that happened to me too. I know exactly how you feel.' And believe that you may have experienced the same feelings as the person you are trying to help. This is called *identification* and is not empathy. In fact it makes empathy more difficult because your own feelings keep getting in the way of your efforts to understand accurately the other person.

I remember feeling very angry with someone who, on the day of my dad's funeral came up to me and said 'I know how you feel, I was in a prisoner of war camp. You've got to be strong and look after your mother.'

In that one phrase they showed me that although they were trying their best to help, they had got it wrong. They just didn't understand how I felt and they hadn't made any effort to. What I wanted (but I didn't know what it was called then) was empathy. Some reaching out to understand or gain insight into my feelings, thoughts and attitudes.

Of course what may have been stopping this person from empathising with me was the fact that they were grieving for my father too. Their own feelings were getting in the way of their efforts to understand me. Not only were they grieving for my father but by their words of 'comfort' to me, it seems likely that my father's death had reminded them of the pain they felt at the loss of their friends in the prisoner of war camp some thirty years before. Not to mention the other terrible ordeals they had to endure then.

This tangle of emotions is not limited to those who have suffered in POW camps. We all have tangles like this just waiting to get activated! This is why self-awareness is so important if we are to try and help others in a straightforward and effective way.

Congruence or genuineness

This involves the helper being open to his or her own feelings as much as possible. It means being my real self - without front or facade, without acting like an 'expert'. Carl Rogers often described it as being 'transparently real' and implicit in the core condition of genuineness is the challenge to us to be ourselves; fallible, vulnerable, imperfect, not knowing any of the answers etc.

This goes against some of the training we might have received in the so-called 'helping professions' which advises us to keep a professional distance, bluff it out, pretend we know what we're doing (even if we don't) and close ranks. Some of this behaviour *might* be useful when trying to help as a nurse, teacher or doctor (although I must say I'm not too sure about this), but it is definitely not part of a counselling way of helping.

Rogers describes genuineness from the client's point of view:

'It has been found that personal change is facilitated when the psychotherapist is what he *is*, when in the relationship with his client he is genuine and without 'front' or facade, openly being the feelings and attitudes which are at that moment flowing *in* him.'
On Becoming a Person, p.61.

This doesn't mean to say that the helper let's her feelings gush out in an uncontrolled torrent all of the time. It means that the helper should first of all not deny or avoid, but be aware of her feelings and then not be afraid of expressing them if appropriate.

From the helper's point of view Rogers writes:

'I have come to recognise that being trustworthy does not demand that I be rigidly consistent but that I be dependably real. The term 'congruent' is one that I have used to describe the way I would like to be. By this I mean that whatever feeling or attitude I am experiencing would be matched by my awareness of that attitude. When this is true, then I am a unified or integrated person in that moment, and hence I can be whatever I deeply am.'
On Becoming a Person, p.50

This means that the whole person is brought to the activity of helping; feelings, thoughts, attitudes, 'warts and all'. We don't just bring a professional expertise, but all of our humanness. Indeed our expertise *is* our humanness, so if we leave that behind, we will not be effective helpers.

Returning to the example of the person at my father's funeral: they could have been congruent, that is to say, aware of their own feelings of grief and the links back to their POW experiences and said: *'Your father's death has taken me right back to the terrible days in the Prisoner of War camp during the second world war. I lost so many friends there. I'm doubly upset because I was close to your father and now I'm reminded of all those years ago.'*

Then I could have seen this person as real, as a person with their own grieving to resolve. They might then have said: *'I can see how upset you are too, it must be terrible for you today, I know how close you were to your dad.'* This last sentence is empathic and would have been much easier for me to hear after the congruent statement above.

Genuineness, then is any expression of the helper's capacity to be in touch with his or her feelings thoughts or even bodily sensations as s/he seeks to understand the client's world of experience.

Unconditional Positive Regard (UPR)

This core condition is also called non-judgemental warmth or acceptance. It means that we must be able to totally accept the person we are trying to help as a worthwhile human being. The helper must be able to believe that each person is worthy, is ok deep down, or 'all right' underneath it all. Seeing someone as worthy does not mean that you have to approve of their behaviour. It simply means that you see them as a human being of equal value.

I rather like the term non-judgemental warmth, since it puts the rather neutral non-judgemental bit next to the very positive 'warmth'. It also helps us break down the core conditions into two component elements; firstly the absence, or suspension of judgement and secondly the positive feeling of warmth, and the communication of this warmth to the person you are helping. Many people come for counselling-style helping because thay have been damaged by other people's harsh, heavy handed, unreasonable or unneccessary judgement. It's important that they don't get more of the same from those trying to help mend the hurts.

Carl Rogers writes:
> 'Can I free him (the client) from the threat of external evaluation? In almost every phase of our lives - at home, at school, at work - we find ourselves under the rewards and punishments of external judgements. "That's good"; "that's naughty." "That's worth an A"; "that's a failure." "That's good counseling"; "that's poor counseling." Such judgements are a part of our lives from infancy to old age.'
> *On Becoming a Person*, p.54.

You may think that an honest evaluation of another person might be quite helpful under some circumstances, and I guess you would be right. Helping styles and roles other than a counselling way of helping could legitimately use judgements in their repertiore of skills. Teachers for example will have to make judgements about a student's work or level of achievement. However, even in this setting, it is important to be careful and respectful in the manner in which the judgement is delivered. In Chapter 3 I looked at the role of feedback in personal development and of course, feedback is a sort of judgement. The difference is that it is not a judgement about the person and their worth, but feedback about their behaviour.

The two core conditions of congruence and UPR do leave us with a dilemma though. There are potential areas of conflict between being non-judgemental and warm whilst simultaneously being genuine. In simple terms the dilemma is this:

> What would happen if you were supposed to be helping someone whom you didn't like because, for example, you knew that they were a convicted rapist?
> • Should you be genuine (and judgemental) and say that you don't like them.
> Or,
> • Should you be non-judgemental and be (falsely) warm and accepting towards them.

This sort of dilemma is often highlighted by introductory courses. It's worthwhile taking a moment to consider how you might resolve this apparent conflict.

Often our worries about not being able to be warm stem from our values or deeply held views. This issue overlaps with personal development, prejudice and the work on personal values we looked at in Chapters 3 and 4. (You might like to remind yourself of the issues we covered there.) This serves to illustrate how central self-awareness and personal development are to learning about counselling and how to do it. You may be tempted to think that you could 'hide' your judgemental attitudes from the person you are working with. There will be opportunities during your course to do some active listening practice, it might be useful task your partner if they think they could see through any pretence. Also, do you think you would be fooled? No matter how desperate for help someone is, they usually still have their 'bullshit detector' switched on.

Here are some other possibilities for you to consider. In each case the question is how do you experience the conflict between genuineness and non-judgemental warmth - is it more important to be non-judgemental, more important to be genuine or is there a way to be both at the same time? What would you do if:

• You were asked to help a young woman who had a problem pregnancy and was considering a termination.

• You were sexually attracted to the person you were trying to help.

• The person you are helping tells you that they were violent to their children when they were young.

• The person you are trying to help says that they have thought of killing themselves.

✎ *YOU MIGHT LIKE TO MAKE YOUR OWN NOTES AT THIS POINT.*

Getting to know the Core Conditions.
(A self-awareness exercise)

Think of each core condition in turn - Empathy, Congruence and Unconditional Positive Regard. For each core condition, think of a person that embodies that core condition. Someone who is the living, breathing personification of that core condition for you. (This should be a real person - someone you know.) Think of a time when you were with this person, perhaps recently, when you 'received' the particular core condition from them.

1. Who is the person - what relationship do you have with them? Write down a brief description of them.

2. What are the qualities of Empathy, Congruence, and UPR that this person conveys?

3. How does it feel to be on the receiving end of each core condition?

EMPATHY IS.....

WHEN I RECEIVE EMPATHY I FEEL......

CONGRUENCE IS.....

WHEN I RECEIVE CONGRUENCE I FEEL......

UPR IS.....

WHEN I RECEIVE UPR I FEEL......

Necessary and Sufficient

When Carl Rogers described the core conditions in 1957, he also said that they were both necessary and sufficient before helpful change was possible.

By **necessary** he meant that helpful change will only happen if all three core conditions are present. If one is missing, change will either not happen or if it does happen, it may not be helpful change. As we noted in Chapter 3 there are many types of change, and some of the core conditions may be present to a greater or lesser degree, but only when all three are present will the change be helpful. It could be said for example, that brainwashing is change - but we would not consider brainwashing to be 'helpful' change. This means that providing a helping relationship can be quite difficult since we have to provide all three core conditions, and they have to be *received* by the person we are trying to help.

By **sufficient** Rogers meant that if all three core conditions are present, then helpful change will take place regardless of any other conditions being met - nothing ekae is necessary. So if the core conditions are provided by accident or in an unplanned manner, helpful change would still take place. Have you ever felt that someone was a 'natural' listener or helper? Someone that was sought out by others to share their troubles with? Such people can probably provide the core conditions quite instinctively, without thinking about it or being trained as a person-centred helper. The exercise on page 60 asks you to identify people who can provide these core conditions singly. Occasionally we meet someone who can provide all three instinctively and we experience them as naturally respectful and understanding; deeply caring and very helpful.

Counselling and helping skills.
The work of Gerard Egan.

The next step in learning about counselling is to see how the core conditions translate into a set of identifiable skills. It isn't enough to just think hard to yourself 'I'm being Empathic, Warm and Genuine' or chant the words like a mantra. The core conditions have to be *experienced by the client* before they are of any use.

Gerard Egan published the first edition of his popular book *The Skilled Helper* in 1975. He added to the ideas of Carl Rogers by taking the work of other psychologists and constructing a theory of helping based on the skills required at different stages in the helpful change process. (Along with others, Egan thinks that the core conditions may be necessary, but are not sufficient - they need some extra elements added to them before helping can be properly effective.)

Many counsellors think that Rogers' ideas were fine as they stood and didn't need anything adding to them - in fact this is my view too. (In short, we think that the core conditions really are necessary and sufficient.) However, for the purposes of learning about counselling and helping, Egan's model of counselling is a very handy way of getting across the idea that certain skills are involved.

At this introductory level of training, you will not have enough time to practise the skills in order to become proficient. This takes a different amount of time for each of us, although counselling skills courses take around one hundred hours over a year and you may wish to continue your training by enrolling for one when you have completed this course. Most people coming to counselling training aready have some of the skills necessary, so it's a case of finding out what your skills are then trying to develop a complete or more rounded repertoire of helping skills. In this book, all we can do is find out what the skills are by briefly identifying them, giving examples and maybe putting them in a context.

Stage I:Building the helping relationship and exploration.

In this first stage, the helper is creating a warm trusting relationship with the client, enabling the client to look at or explore whatever they choose. The helper is trying to step into the other person's shoes and look at the world form the client's point of view.

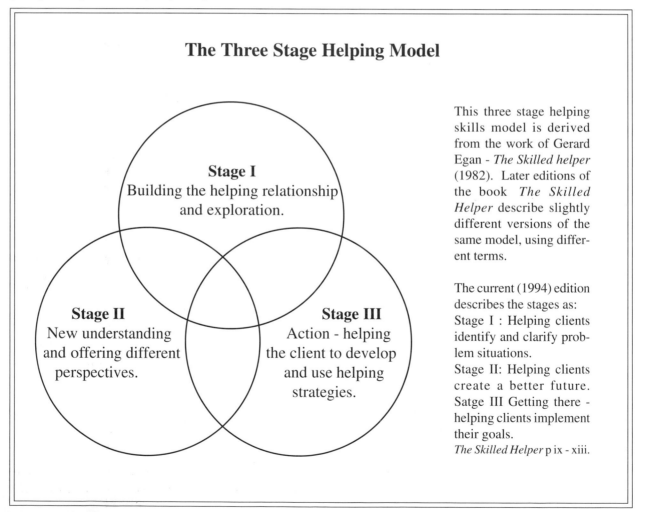

The Three Stage Helping Model

Stage I
Building the helping relationship and exploration.

Stage II
New understanding and offering different perspectives.

Stage III
Action - helping the client to develop and use helping strategies.

This three stage helping skills model is derived from the work of Gerard Egan - *The Skilled helper* (1982). Later editions of the book *The Skilled Helper* describe slightly different versions of the same model, using different terms.

The current (1994) edition describes the stages as:
Stage I : Helping clients identify and clarify problem situations.
Stage II: Helping clients create a better future.
Satge III Getting there - helping clients implement their goals.
The Skilled Helper p ix - xiii.

Stage I Skills This first stage incorporates Rogers' core conditions of empathy, congruence and UPR. The specific skills associated with this stage are:

- developing a trusting relationship:
  - making and maintaining contact,
  - structuring,
  - communicating non-judgemental warmth,
  - communicating genuineness.

- active listening and communicating empathy:
  - identifying, acknowledging and reflecting thoughts, behaviours and feelings,
  - paraphrasing,
  - clarifying.

We will look at these Stage I skills in more detail below under the heading 'Basic Skills for Basic Helping', where I will explain each skill and give examples.

Stage II Skills In this stage the client is helped to see themselves and their life from new perspectives, taking into consideration alternative information and other viewpoints. This is done using all of Stage I skills, plus:

- Linking and integrating individual issues and problems into themes:
  - showing deeper understanding and empathy
  - helping the client focus on specific issues.

- Challenging the client's views:
  - offering new perspectives,
  - sharing the helper's experiences and feelings,
  - helping the client move on.

- Goal setting:
  - helping the client identify what they want achieve.

Stage III Skills Now the helper is trying to look, with the client, at possible ways of acting in the situation to help resolve the problem. Possible outcomes will be considered and risks assessed. The client will then be helped to evaluate the effectiveness of their new behaviour. This is achieved using all of Stage I and II skills, plus:

- Helping the client move on to considering action.

- Developing and choosing action plans:
  - brainstorming,
  - creative thinking,
  - problem solving,
  - decision making,
  - planning.

Evaluating consequences of actions:
  - recording events, e.g. diary keeping,
  - evaluation,
  - reviewing plans.

As the client progresses through the stages proposed by Egan, the emphasis shifts from the client's point of view and their world to a more objective perspective and finally action in and on the client's world to cause change. This may seem far removed from Carl Rogers' ideas of the innate self-healing process. Egan expresses his understanding of the client's ability to direct their own helping process by having the helper as a co-worker, making suggestions or offering ways of tackling issues which the client can use or not as *they* choose.

Rogerian Person-Centred counsellors let the client discover their own new perspectives and make their own action plans by helping the client activate their own self-healing process. The counsellor does this by providing the core conditions almost exclusively through Stage I skills.

Basic Helping

This extensive range of skills that are used in counselling takes a long time to properly develop, as we shall see Chapter 11. In this book we can do only a little more than list the skills.

In Chapter 1 I coined the phrase 'helping in a counselling way' to describe the basic counselling-style helping that uses a counselling approach, but not a full range of properly developed counselling skills. Helping in a counselling way does not use the professional or ethical framework that counsellors use either, but those using this basic helping in a counselling way will have at least considered the positive effects of, for example, the boundaries of helping relationships, see Chapter 1.

Basic Skills for Basic Helping

There are some skills fundamental to the helping process that you might like to practise as part of your basic helping. These are the Stage I Skills listed above. You will probably spend an hour or two on your introductory course finding out how difficult it actually is, even though the skills themselves sound quite simple. The ingredients for skills training are repeated practice, evaluation and feedback. If you want to practise skills you will need to set up a situation in which you can get these ingredients.

You may get together with colleagues from your course or try it out with friends.

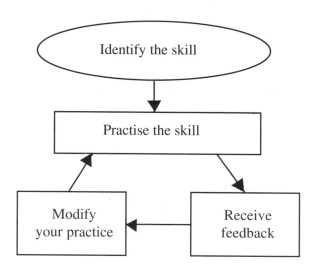

The most difficult ingredient to get right in such informal 'training' arrangements is feedback. In Chapter 3 I looked at feedback in a little more detail in the context of personal development. In a skills training setting it is just as important to be accurate in your observations and honest in your feedback. Since the core conditions have to be communicated to the client, it is the client or, as is sometimes the case in skills training, the person in the client role, whose feedback is most valuable. It is common practice to have a third person acting as an observer who can give the counsellor/helper feedback from a more objective position seeing as they were not on the receiving end of the skills.

Feedback in training is helpful then, if it comes from two sources; firstly the client or person being helped or listened to, and secondly a 'neutral' observer.

Developing Stage I Skills

● *Developing a trusting relationship:*
  1. Making and maintaining contact.
  2. Structuring.

Every relationship happens in a series of episodes, that is the times the people concerned actually meet and make contact (this could of course, be on the 'phone or by letter, but we will only concern ourselves with face-to-face meetings here). A relationship begins with the first meeting or episode and the first 'task' in the first episode is to work out what kind or type of relationship it is going to be. This happens pretty quickly and will depend upon the setting, the roles that the people are in, their expectations and the first things that are said. It is called '*structuring*':

(College class room)
  'Hello, my name is Pete Sanders and I'll be teaching you GCSE maths this year.'

(Telephone)
  'Hello, Samaritans, can I help?'

(Student services in college)
  'Hello, my name is Pete, I'm a counsellor here. You must be Sandra. I don't know why you've come to the counselling service, but I'll do my best to help in whatever way I can. Would you like to tell me what's concerning you?'

(Street)
  'Excuse me, could you tell me how to get to the station?'

(Bank)
  'Don't make a noise or raise the alarm. This is a gun under my coat. Now give me the money! MOVE!'

Some of these are helping relationships and some are not. We can tell because of the setting, the roles, the expectations of the situation or by what is said. How would you make contact in a way that indicates you are offerring help?
✍

After you've made contact in a helping relationship, the next task is to maintain that contact. This is done by doing certain things (non-verbal communication) and saying certain things or making noises (you don't have to actually say words). What are the methods of maintaining contact that you use?

VERBAL METHODS

SAYING 'YES' 'I SEE' 'PLEASE GO ON'
'RIGHT' 'UH-HUH' 'MMMM'
✍ ....

NON-VERBAL METHODS

LOOKING AT THE PERSON   SMILING
NODDING   MAKING EYE CONTACT
LEANING FORWARD IN YOUR CHAIR
✍ ....

Once again, a flipchart from our imaginary group shows some possible answers. Do you have any to add?

The things we do and say to keep in contact with another person come quite naturally to most of us. In a helping relationship, however, we want to communicate warmth, genuineness and empathy even in the way we say 'I see'. Whether we are successful can only be determined by asking for feedback.

- *Developing a trusting relationship:*
    - ***3. Communicating non-judgemental warmth.***
    - ***4. Communicating genuineness.***

Both verbal and non-verbal methods of communication figure strongly in this next section too. Communicating non-judgemental warmth and genuineness is as much about *what you do* as *what and how you say* something. Most of us that are attracted to a counselling way of helping tend to be less judgemental than average, but it can still be a difficult task. It's obvious that if you're striving to be non-judgemental in a counselling way, you don't say:

> "Don't you know that having an abortion is killing another human being and is only done by bad, evil people?"

However, many of us do have strong feelings about abortion and may well feel something similar. The question is how do you accept someone who is behaving in an unacceptable way? It is necessary firstly to separate the person and their intrinsic worth as a human being from their behaviour, which may be unacceptable. Then secondly be aware of your own values and prejudices and be willing to suspend them and withhold judgement for the time being as the person you are helping strives to change. Of course they may not change in a way in which you think is sensible. Skills specific to being accepting are:

Be specific, avoid generalising:
Say: 'It sounds as though it was really painful for you when your father died.'
Don't say: 'Everyone feels bad when someone close to them dies, it's only natural.'

Don't debate things - you're not having a discussion, you're trying to help:
Say: 'So you think it would be best if you went to the Clinic for advice on contraception.'
Don't say: 'I wouldn't go to the clinic, the best place to go is your GP, they know your medical history.'

Don't push the person you are trying to help too far or too fast - accept their pace:
Say: 'It seems as though you don't want to go any further with this at the moment.'
Don't say: ' You've spent a long time talking about this topic, don't you think it is time you moved on to what's really upsetting you.'

Don't make guesses or interpretations - you're no expert on the client's troubles:
Say: 'So you think that the time your boss overlooked you for promotion was the start of this low patch.'
Don't say: 'Well, you say your boss is responsible, but it sounds as though it's more likely to be the fact that your mother died last year.'

Each one of the 'Don't say' responses above is non-accepting or judgemental in some way. For example:

'Everyone feels bad when someone close to them dies, it's only natural.'

This sounds caring and possibly helpful, but the hidden judgemental message is something like:

'Your hurt isn't specially bad because this sort of thing happens to everybody.'

It might be useful to try to identify the 'hidden judgements' behind the other responses and you may know of some other ways of being judgemental which helpers might wish to avoid.

✍

- *Active listening and communicating empathy:*
  1. Identifying, acknowledging and reflecting thoughts, behaviours and feelings.

Active listening is one of the key ingredients in any helping relationship. It is impossible to be helpful if you are not actively listening. Active listening means that you have to attend to all of the signals given off by a person - not only the sounds, but using your sight to pick up the non-verbal signals. It should really be called 'active attention' because we are trying to actively pay the most detailed and special attention to the other person using all our senses.

The purpose of this active listening is to pay attention to, and try to understand, the thoughts, feelings and behaviour of the other person. How do we do this? If you were the helper, what would you be paying attention to in the speech and behaviour of the other person?

> ACTIVE LISTENING - WHAT WE PAY ATTENTION TO IN THE PERSON WE ARE HELPING
>
> VOICE QUALITY - SOFT, HARD, CONFIDENT, TIMID, STRONG, WEAK, ETC.
> BREATHING - DEEP, SHALLOW, SOBBING, SNATCHED, RELAXED, ETC.
> FACIAL EXPRESSION - RELAXED, TENSE, AFRAID, HAPPY, DISGUST, ETC.
> WHETHER THEY ARE TALKING OR SILENT.
> THE 'STORY' THEY ARE TELLING.
>
> ✍ ....

On the flipchart above, our imaginary group have come up with some suggestions to start off. How do their ideas compare with your own, the list is not complete by any means.

There are three stages to the skill of active listening (the arrows indicate the flow of information):

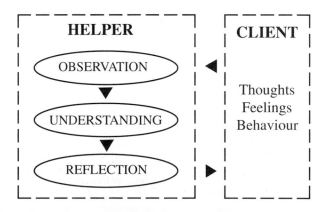

After paying close attention to the other person, comes understanding the meaning of what you are seeing and hearing. In order to do this you need to have achieved some degree of self-awareness. We find it easier to understand another person if we:

- Suspend our judgement of the other person.
- Put our own feelings and experiences to one side while we are trying to understand theirs.
- Try to put ourselves in their shoes and see the world form their point of view.

The final test to see if we do really understand the world of meanings of the other person in all it's subtlety, is to check with them. We do this by *reflection, paraphrasing and clarifying.* Reflection is the basic skill and at its most simple involves reflecting the content of the other person's utterances back to them. The purpose is to give the message :
I am listening carefully to what you're saying and I am trying to understand. I will demonstrate this to you by letting you know that I heard what you just said. Did I get it right?'

The ability to give good reflections without sounding like a parrot is a matter of practice until the activity becomes natural to *you.*

- *Active listening and communicating empathy:*
  2. Paraphrasing,
  3. Clarifying.

Paraphrasing and clarifying come hot on the heels of reflection and constitute the three basic skills of the core condition of empathy. When used together they become a powerful method of communicating your care and attention for the person you are trying to help.

Paraphrasing: is summarising in a few words what the speaker is saying. Depending upon the circumstances, it may be best to use the client's own words or use your own words. It is a matter of judgement to know how best to paraphrase depending upon the situation. In order to paraphrase effectively we need a reasonable vocabulary, especially when it comes to putting feelings into words. For this reason, I have included the 'feelings vocabulary' activity on the page opposite.

Clarifying: is not quite as obvious as it sounds. It doesn't mean that you clarify the client's muddled thinking, or can see more sense in the client's world than they can. Both of these are rather arrogant positions to be in and would probably be experienced by them as very unaccepting and superior. Rather, it means seeking clarification of your own understanding of the client's world. This can have a number of helpful effects:

1. The client will feel that you're trying really hard to understand.
2. You will get a better, more accurate understanding of the client's world.
3. The client may come to understand themselves better as a consequence of having to explain something in more detail, or in a different way to you.
4. Sometimes when a client is in a muddle or fog, you may pick this up by feeling muddled yourself. If you ask for clarification *for yourself*, it can help your client clarify their own thoughts and feelings.

Developing a 'Feelings Vocabulary'

Because some of us may not be used to being very expressive where feelings are concerned, we may not have a very large vocabulary of words which we use to describe feelings. It can be very useful to build up the vocabulary of feelings words we use. This is a brainstorming activity for small groups, but you can start it off yourself and then ask your friends to make contributions. Simply think of all the feeling words you know and write them down. You may find that some of the words are alternatives, or indicating a subtle difference in feeling. You could try to group them together under headings if you find it helpful. Then, start using them more often to help you get some 'colour' and richness into your descriptions of feelings.

Angry	Sad	Happy	Hurt	Afraid
annoyed	unhappy	elated	upset	scared
enraged	gloomy	cheery	broken	hesitant
cross	choked up	glad	suffering	insecure
sulky	sullen	festive	crushed	panicky
irate	flat	merry	tortured	terrified
belligerent	mournful	jubilant	heartbroken	shaky
....	....	....	....	....

Words about intimacy

loving
tender
close
sexual
in-tune
seductive
....

Words about interest

curious
fascinated
inquisitive
attentive
enthusiastic
absorbed
....

Other feeling words

envious
jealous
bored
bold
proud
excited
....

Use your 'feelings vocabulary' in pairs on your course .

That completes the expanded list of Stage I skills, and as I suggested earlier, it is not appropriate to elaborate the skills associated with Stages II and II any further. There will be hardly any time to practice skills on an introductory course, this activity is given priority on Certificate and Counselling Skills courses. You may, however wish to use what course time you do get profitably, in which case the following suggestions may be useful if followed with your tutor's more detailed instructions.

Practising and Integrating Stage I Skills

It's one thing separating out the Stage I counselling skills for the purposes of illustrating each one; it's quite another to put them back together into a natural piece of real-life helping. I have been at pains to point out that an introduction to counselling course does not prepare or qualify anyone to do any counselling or use counselling skills other than inform the natural basic helping we all do as colleagues, friends and relatives.

If you do want to practise these helping skills with a colleague, friend or course participant, start off by taking one skill at a time. When you have practised one at a time, you may like to try putting them together in twos and threes. It may help to try them in the order found in this chapter, since this is roughly the order in which the skills are found in an actual relationship.

Never forget that, when practising skills in this way, your prime aim is to learn something. Don't get carried away and begin believing that it is a real helping session. You must make sure that you and your friend feel safe enough to talk and listen freely. Make sure you set some ground-rules before you start:

• Are you going to make up a story and play the part of someone else or are you going to be yourselves, talking about your own real issues?

• If you are going to talk about real issues, is the practice session confidential?

• Practice is no good without feedback - how are you going to get it?

• It might help to list the skills on a piece of paper and then check them off at the end to indicate those that were appropriately present in the practise session.

I do not recommend 'practising' counselling skills on unsuspecting friends and relatives. Never use others as unconsenting guinea-pigs. It is neither ethical nor respectful, so is automatically an unacceptable way of improving your skills. You will find, however, that quite naturally your interpersonal behaviour will change, probably without you realising it. Others may notice and comment. If they do, it might be worth asking them what the changes are and whether they think it is an improvement. All feedback is useful!

What To Do When You Reach Your Limits

When we are helping others in a counselling way, these helping relationships can begin and end in different ways. One particular beginning and ending event in helping that happens whether you are a counsellor, using counselling skills or helping in a counselling way is called *referral*. Many trainers in counselling will be wondering why there is a chapter on referrals in a book aimed at basic introductory courses. The answer is that referrals don't only happen in professional settings.

• You don't have to be a professional counsellor in order for another helper or agency to refer a client to you for helping.

•Similarly you may be trying to help a friend or a colleague at work with a problem and think that it might be better if someone else helps them rather than you.

It doesn't matter whether you are a professional or a volunteer, qualified or unqualified, making and receiving referrals should be done with the utmost care and consideration for the person you are helping/ counselling.

Receiving a referral is when:
   • Someone is recommended to see you for helping/counselling by the helper/counsellor they are currently seeing.

• A client comes to see you after deciding themselves that you are the helper/counsellor that they want to see. (This is called *self-referral*.)

Making a referral is when:
   •You feel that the person you are helping/ counselling would be better helped by another helper/counsellor.
   • Your client feels that they want help/ counselling from someone other than you.

There are many reasons why we have to pass people on from one helper to another and all of the reasons are to do with *limits* of one sort or another. Here is a list of some of the limits involved (there may be some of your own that I haven't thought of). When you see this symbol:

✍ *MAKE A NOTE OF YOUR OWN, ADDITIONAL IDEAS:*

• Limits of the situation:
   legal limits
   service/agency limits
   limits of counselling itself
   time/timetable limits
   ✍ ....

• My personal limits:
   confidence limits
   emotional limits
   ✍ ....

• The limits of my competence:
>   no expertise in specialist area
>   skills limits
>   qualification limits
>
>   ✍ ....

• The limits of the person I am helping/counselling:
>   lack of confidence in me
>   doesn't like me
>   wanting a different style of helping
>   wanting a different type of helper e.g. male,
>   female, gay, black, white etc
>
>   ✍ ....

It's possible in our enthusiasm for helping people that we try to help everyone, in every situation, all of the time, regardless of their problem. This way of working is always dangerous. It's obvious that no-one can do this, but it's easy to get seduced into thinking that we can.
>   • Sometimes it happens *because the people we are trying to help expect it of us.*
>   • Sometimes it happens *because we expect it of ourselves.*
>   • Sometimes it happens *because our boss tell us that we must do it* - or at least suggests that it's the done thing if you want to get on.

It's dangerous to work beyond our limits because:
>   • Beyond our limits we cannot be of any help, we will probably *do damage to the person we are trying to help.*
>   • Beyond our limits we will put stress on ourselves and probably *do damage to ourselves.*

>   • Beyond our limits we will be seen as acting irresponsibly and *do damage to the reputation of helping or counselling or the agency we work for.*

In order to avoid working beyond our limits we need to understand where those limits are. It will be a little early in your learning about counselling for most of you reading this book to think too deeply about what your limits might be, but it's important to know that as helpers of any kind we must know our limits and stay within them.

We will look at each of these sets of limits in a little more detail, but before we do it's important to remember that with referrals, as with everything else in a counselling way of helping:
• each situation is different, each client unique, and each requires special consideration leading to its *own* solution.

We will tackle the problem of understanding limits by asking some questions. By now you will realise that the questions we ask in training in counselling do not always have fixed right or wrong answers. They're much more interesting than that - there's room for opinion, discussion and disagreement. These questions are no exception. When you see this symbol:

✍ *MAKE A NOTE OF YOUR ANSWERS & EXAMPLES*

Understanding the limits of the situation
>   • Are there any legal requirements which mean that I cannot help this person?
>   *Examples: it may be illegal to offer certain kinds of help to children - e.g. issue*

contraceptives or advice about family planning. It is currently illegal to help someone to commit suicide.

✍

• Does my agency have a policy which prevents me from helping this person?
Examples: An alcohol counselling service may not help someone unless they stay 'dry'. A women's counselling centre may not help male clients or people who have undergone a sex change operation from male to female.

✍

• Counselling cannot help everyone in every situation. Am I trying to use a counselling way of helping in a situation in which it cannot be effective?
Example: Counselling is ineffective in solving 'concrete' problems like being homeless or having no money because you're unemployed or being denied a service because you're disabled or being refused admission because you're black. (Counselling can help to make people feel stronger, less trodden down and more worthwhile as a person, but can't get you a house, a job or human rights.)

✍

• Do I have enough time to help this person effectively?
Examples: Someone may want help when it's inconvenient - during your lunch hour or five minutes before you're due to go off duty or

when all appointments for the week are filled. What would you do in these situations?

✍

Understanding my personal limits
• What 'tender spots' do I have emotionally? (See Chapter 3.)
Examples: Some people say that they could not work with, for example, rapists or abusers. You may feel very emotionally sensitive to certain situations after recent upsets, e.g. bereavement.

✍

• How confident in my helping abilities and skills am I?
Examples: I might be overconfident in my ability to help someone because I've been told by my friends that I'd make a brilliant counsellor or, I might be frightened of trying to help someone in case I mess it up, even though I have the necessary skills.

✍

Understanding the limits of my competence
• Does this person need help in a specialist area that I know little or nothing about?
Examples: Clients might need medical attention, welfare rights information or help from a specialist counsellor, i.e. drug rehabilitation counsellor.

✍

• How far do my helping skills go?
Examples: It would not be appropriate to try to help distressed or disturbed people with only a smattering of rudimentary skills. Counselling is a skilled and ethical profession requiring lengthy training. If you think your skills are not up to it - you're almost certainly right. Get ready to refer your client on.

Your client may need what Steve Williams (1993) calls 'formal' help. By this he means help provided by statutory services such as the health service, social services etc. How will you know if your client needs this kind of help?

• What do my qualifications permit me to do?
Examples: Obviously only doctors can make a medical diagnosis, but you'd be surprised the number of times clients expect you to either be a doctor or be able to give them medical advice, like how many tablets to take or why their baby is crying. Clients may ask for all kinds of advice from helpers. If you give advice you're not qualified to and something goes wrong, you or your agency may be liable.

Lack of qualifications should not stop you from helping within your limits. The best sort of helping you can offer is *accurate active listening*. This will be a novel experience for many people seeking help

---

What is Formal Help?

'When using the term 'formal' I am talking about the whole pattern of statutory services that are available to help individuals whose emotional distress is so pronounced that they would seriously stretch the resources of any counsellor'
Steve Williams: *An Incomplete Guide to Referral Issues for Counsellors*, p.44

If you are helping in a counselling way you may be either on your own - helping in your family, community or at work, or working - paid or voluntary- for a service or agency. It is important to know that your helping should not extend to very disturbed people without backup. An agency or service can provide this backup in the form of support or medical advice on hand. If you are on your own, there's no need to feel completely isolated. GPs, social workers or in an emergency the casualty department of your local hospital (often called Accident and Emergency Dept) are all there to help and support you if you are trying to help a relative or friend. Do not try to 'go it alone', professional counsellors have backup *and use it*. So everyone who is helping in a counselling way should be ready to pass the person they are helping on to those more skilled, qualified or able to help.

How do you know if the person you are helping needs formal help?

Persistent symptoms: if I have symptoms such as physical sensations, breathlessness or pains, sleep disturbances or eating problems which persist more than a week or so, they are common symptoms of grief or anxiety. Talking the problem through will help and the symptoms should ease after a short time. If they persist, get yourself backup and me some professional help - my GP is best.

Unusual or **extreme** symptoms: hearing voices in my head, thinking that someone is controlling my thoughts, seeing things that aren't there are all unusual symptoms which must be drawn to the attention of my GP. Extreme depression or fear which makes it impossible for me to go out of my house also mean that I should see my doctor. If you notice that I am harming myself by cutting or burning myself or if I threaten to kill myself, again, I should be encouraged to see my doctor.

What to do

Ask me if it's alright if you contact my doctor or social worker. Ask me if I want you to come along to give me moral support. You could encourage me to go and check up to see if I kept the appointment.

- to be sensitively listened to is deeply comforting. It will also have the added benefit of assisting you to make the decision as to whether your client needs any more highly qualified help.

Understanding my client's limits

The next type of limit also needs some active listening from you. Your task is to understand why your client wants to be referred on, since sometimes a client themselves will identify the need for referral. The questions that follow do not require answers from your point of view. They might, however, give you some idea of the reasons that clients wish to be referred on to another helper. Make a note of any reasons you come up with yourself.

• Does my client lack confidence in my ability?

• Does this client dislike me?
There is no rule that says we must be able to be liked by all of our clients. Some people just don't hit it off from the moment they meet. Such instant dislike would inevitable get in the way of the client being able to receive help from you.

• Does this client require a different style of helping?
Your way of helping, whether it's your own personal style or the counselling approach that you use, may not suit the person you are

helping. They might find it too laid back or maybe too intrusive.

• Does the person you are helping want a different type of helper?

✍

When not to make a referral

In his book An Incomplete Guide to Referral Issues for Counsellors, Steve Williams pointed out that whenever we consider referring a client on to another helper we must make sure we know **when not to make a referral.** By this he means that we should carefully consider our motives for making or receiving a referral. What possibly questionable motives could there be?

• You don't like a client very much and you would rather refer them on because cannot bring yourself to say so.

• A client's problem is awkward to handle, so you would rather refer them to another helper than sort out the awkward problem.

• A client is inconvenient, so you would rather refer them on than bear the inconvenience.

✍ You might like to write down any more motives that could be behind your own referrals.

As we learned in Chapter 5, one of the 'core' conditions of a counselling way of helping is *genuineness* or *congruence*. This core condition requires us to be open about our feelings and reasons for doing things. It might be better to be honest and open about our feelings towards the person we are trying to help, rather than trying to avoid the feelings by off-loading the client to someone else. See Chapter 8 on *Support and Supervision in Counselling* for more help with this.

Making a referral: How to do it.

Having looked at the 'whys and why-nots' of making referrals, the question is, how do you do it? Most people would think that it's just a matter of passing your client on and that the process should be simple and obvious. Even if this is the case (*I* don't think it is quite that simple), *helping in a counselling way is often about understanding and refining the art of the obvious.*

Steve Williams (1993) suggests a checklist which I have adapted for our use. As soon as the possibility of making a referral occurs to you, go through the checklist to explore what action you feel it would be appropriate to take:

• Has anything been said about referral yet?

• Who has identified the need for referral?
> Me.
> The person I am helping.

• What is the purpose of the referral?
> To get properly qualified help.
> To get more expert help.
> So that I don't go beyond my limits.
> Different type of helper wanted.
> Different style of helper wanted.
> Any other purposes.....

• Do I have enough information about possible referral agencies? If not, do I know how to go about getting it?

• What do I want to say to my client?

• What backup or support do I need for this referral?

✍ You might like to write down any more checklist ideas that might aid your own referrals.

At the heart of each onward referral lie the following aims:

• To pass the person on as though they were a precious gift rather than an awkward bundle.

• To pass the person on so that their life and experience is added to rather than taken away from.

• To make sure the person understands that the 'passing on' that I'm doing is not a rejection of them, but my best attempt to help them meet their needs better.

• To make sure that the person knows that they will be welcome to seek help from me or the agency I am working for in the future, at which point I will again do my best to help them meet their needs.

✍ You might like to write down any more aims you might have for your own referrals.

Receiving referrals

It can be a great feeling to be asked to help someone. They may come along themselves (a self-referral) or someone else may suggest that they come to see you. It's flattering to think that someone thinks you might be able to help. It's easy to get caught up in the good feelings and say 'Yes of course I can!' before you've thought about it.

*If your only training is this introductory course then you will have to think very hard before offerring help **since you are not qualified to offer help**.* This may be a problem if your employer has sent you on this course and expects you to go back to your workplace and act as 'the counsellor'. You should point out to your employer that you are not qualified to counsel people and the tutor on your introductory course will support you with that explanation.

If you are working as a volunteer or in a service where you do take referrals to help people in a counselling way, you must be sure you can figure out if the person being referred to you falls within the range you can help. If you work as a volunteer in a drug project - is their problem a drug problem?

Are you prepared to see clients who are sent to you against their will? This sometimes happens if you are, for example, a tutor in a school or college - students may be sent to you because they are not attending their course - yet you may still wish to use a counselling way of helping.

Finally, you must be prepared to say no. This can be difficult because we all like to think we can help others, but you must not get out of your depth. Both you and the person you are trying to help will suffer.

Ethics and Counselling

7

Why bother with ethics at an introductory level?
Not for the first time do I find myself having to explain the inclusion in this introductory text of an area of knowledge which is seen as the responsibility of higher level training. The purpose of this Chapter is twofold; firstly to let readers know of the effort put into the development of ethical frameworks by the counselling profession. We are, of course, all potential clients and the BAC Codes of Ethics & Practice are there to inform and reassure all clients who seek the help of counsellors and helpers who are members of BAC.

Secondly, I am keen to cultivate an attitude of responsible helping regardless of the perceived level of the helping activity. I do not subscribe to the view that 'low level', voluntary, community-based or otherwise amateur helping should be seen as beyond morals, not worthy of rules of conduct, or somehow not important enough for ethics.

The question is 'How should the issue of ethical behaviour be interpreted at this level of *basic helping* or *helping in a counselling way*?' We'll never find out unless and until we have a go at identifying the issues, so this chapter is a starting point for beginning helpers and their trainers.

Ethics - What are they and what are they for?
Ethics can be defined as a set of moral principles or rules of conduct. Most people are familiar with the idea of ethics in medical practice; that doctors must keep their patients' details confidential, and must always act to save or extend life. These and other rules of conduct for doctors are enshrined in the Hippocratic Oath.

Our appreciation of medical ethics is sharpened because doctors deal literally with life and death, and it is when life and death decisions are made that we seek the support of a good set of rules. That is why there is such vigorous debate over such issues as whether to turn off life-support machines, should terminally ill people be 'assisted' to die or at what age is a human foetus considered 'alive', etc. Many of these ethical decisions have a direct relationship with our values, spiritual beliefs, political views and other deeply held convictions.

The profession of counselling has its own 'rules of conduct' and in the UK they have been in a process of development through the professional body, the British Association for Counselling (BAC) since before the first Code of Ethics and Practice for Counsellors was published in 1984. Although counselling and helping doesn't concern itself directly with life-and-death decisions in the same way as medicine, there are several ethical dilemmas which counsellors and helpers can find themselves caught up in. This is because counselling concerns itself with damaged, distressed, or otherwise vulnerable people. From my own experience of needing help, I know that in some desperate circumstances I would do almost anything, to put an end to my distress. At such moments, the 'rules of conduct' or ethics of the helper, whether they are a doctor, lawyer or counsellor, will go some way to protect my interests as a client.

Ethics in Counselling and Helping
The British Association for Counselling publish four codes of ethics and practice:

Code of Ethics & Practice for Counsellors - for those working as counsellors to follow and to help clients understand the conduct they should expect from their counsellor.
Code of Ethics & Practice for Counselling Skills - for those not working as counsellors, but who use counselling skills alongside other professional skills in a helping role other than 'counsellor'. Also to help clients understand the conduct required of their helper.
Code of Ethics & Practice for the Supervision of Counsellors - for those who provide supervision and support to counsellors and for counsellors seeking supervision.
Code of Ethics & Practice for Trainers - for those offering training in counselling and to help people looking for training in counselling know good practice in the conduct of trainers.

All are obtainable from the British Association for Counselling along with other information sheets relating to ethical practice. The BAC address can be found at the back of this book.

It is clear that one code of ethics and practice is not sufficient to cover all of the BAC members' interests and professional activities. Codes of ethics in counselling and helping is very much a matter of 'horses for courses'. Different types and levels of helping activity have different ethical requirements. If we want to understand what ethical considerations we might wish to take into account as beginning helpers offering basic helping in a counselling way, we could start by looking at the ethical framework developed by professional counsellors.

My first suggestion is that you obtain copies of the BAC Codes of Ethics and Practice for Counsellors, Counselling Skills and Trainers (details above). In addition to helping understand the BAC perspective on ethical issues, they will be a useful resource for the future should you or any of your friends or colleagues seek counselling or training. You will know what kind of conduct to expect from counsellors, helping professionals using counselling skills and trainers.

What topics do you think should be covered in a code of ethics for counsellors? Often, when left to our own devices, we get as far as confidentiality and damaging clients, then dry up. After many years of continual development, the main issues considered by the BAC in their codes of ethics and practice are divided into sub-headings including the following:

• Issues of competence:
   Do I have enough training?
   Do I have enough personal and other resources?
   Do I monitor my competence? e.g. through supervision.
   What am I doing to stay effective? e.g. further training, support and supervision?

- Confidentiality:
    What should limit the confidentiality I offer to clients?

- Issues of responsibility:
    What responsibilities to I have towards my clients?,
    What are my responsibilities to myself as a counsellor?
    Do I have any responsibilities to other counsellors and other helping professionals?
    What are my responsibilities to the wider community?

- Advertising:
    How should I advertise any help that I can offer?

These headings are included for information and to stimulate thinking and debate regarding ethical issues. It is not appropriate to go into the BAC Codes of Ethics and Practice in further detail here. That is more properly the business of counselling skills courses and books, and counsellor training courses and their associated texts. However, each of these headings is of relevance to basic helping in a counselling way.

Basic Ethics for Basic Helping

Every time that we offer help to someone, we should consider the way we conduct ourselves. Throughout this book there have been pointers to the issues:
In Chapter 1 we asked: 'What sort of help are we offering?'
In Chapter 2 we asked: 'What gives us the idea that our helping will be effective?'

In Chapter 3 we asked: 'What are our motives for helping?' and 'Will our own feelings and thoughts get in the way?'
In Chapter 4 we asked: 'Do we have any prejudices which will bias our help?'
In Chapter 5 we asked: 'How do we improve our helping skills?'
In Chapter 6 we asked: 'Will we keep within the limits of our expertise?'
In Chapter 8 we will ask: 'Do we have enough personal support to offer effective help without hurting ourselves or those we are trying to help?'

You may see some similarity between the issues raised in the chapters and those included in the BAC codes. They might be considered to be the 'core ethical issues' of *competent and responsible helping practice*. The answers arrived at as you work through this book will have a strong personal element because, as I have pointed out, ethics are to some extent based on our personal values and beliefs. There are, however, some common strands to ethical conduct:

- We try to act within the law.
- We respect human rights.
- We respect people's autonomy and ability to control their own destiny.
- We keep contracts or agreements we have made with those we are trying to help, however informal.
- We try to act in a fair and reasonable way.
- When faced with a dilemma we try to do the most good and the least harm.

If there is any central strand which draws together these ethical issues, it is the welfare of the person we are trying to help. Underneath it all helpers are trying to help someone rather than exploit them; to increase someone's options not narrow them down; to help someone make emancipated autonomous decisions not to manipulate them into doing what we want. We find that these ethical issues also manifest themselves in the kind of basic helping that we might be involved in at an introductory level. For example, if we were to help a colleague at work, or our next door neighbour, we should not abdicate ethical or moral responsibility. We should do our best to ensure good ethical conduct.

How might you behave unethically in the case of helping your colleague at work? Although you are not a trained counsellor, a colleague has come to you for support because his wife has just left him. It was a sudden and unexpected separation and he is distraught. How might you behave unethically?

✍ MAKE A NOTE OF YOUR OWN ANSWERS & EXAMPLES

The greatest danger is that the person you are trying to help is exploited by you either wittingly or unwittingly, for example:

• In your enthusiasm to help, you may help more than you are qualified to,
e.g. you might give him some of your mother's sleeping tablets to help him sleep.

• You may exploit your colleague for personal gain,
e.g. you may see an opportunity for promotion and break confidentiality by telling your boss that your colleague's work is suffering.

• Your own problems might get in the way,
e.g. you may identify very strongly with his problem because of a recent separation of your own. This may lead you to suggest solutions you wish you had tried yourself, rather than ones which might genuinely benefit him in his situation.

• You may have a vested interest in a particular outcome,
e.g. you believe that families should stay together for the sake of the children and try your best to manipulate a reconciliation against everyone's wishes.

• As he turns to you for comfort, in his distress he muddles care and help with sexual attraction and you have a sexual relationship.

Quite clearly these ways of acting will not be in the best interests of the person you are trying to help. There are many more ways of behaving unethically in this situation. You may be working as a volunteer in a helping service already. Do you have a code of conduct? If you think it would be helpful, why not draw up your own set of guidelines for ethical conduct in basic helping.

The question of monitoring the conduct of helpers is partly dealt with in Chapter 8. Any code of practice must carry sanctions with it in those cases where it is broken. There is a complaints procedure operated by the BAC for the benefit of clients, supervisees and trainees. Where basic helping is concerned however, there is no governing body to protect us. Everyone doing basic helping must assume the mantle of responsibility to help in a principled and ethical way.

Support and Supervision in Counselling

Support

Most of us nowadays are familiar with the idea of support. Many people recognise that human beings need various types of support in order to function effectively. Whether you are a single parent, business executive or volunteer, you will understand the need for support. When you see this symbol:

✍ *MAKE A NOTE OF YOUR OWN, OR ADDITIONAL IDEAS*

There are various ways of looking at support:

- *Physical support*: crutches or a plaster cast on a broken limb, holding someone up when they're weak or unwell, using your physical presence as support by going along with someone to the doctor's for example.
- *Verbal support*: speaking up in agreement with someone, being an advocate for someone unable to state their case.
- *Financial support*: a loan for a business venture, a grant for a charity, social security benefits.
- *Emotional support*: a shoulder to cry on, someone to share your troubles with, someone 'rooting' for you during exams, someone believing in you.
- Other support ✍

We've all received support of some kind or another in our lives and would probably have failed without support at some time. Why might helpers need support? ✍

Burnout

Any person's ability to help in a counselling way needs to be maintained rather like a car needs to be maintained between journeys. The oil and water need checking along with the tyre pressure, and we need to make sure there is enough fuel in the tank. We need to assure ourselves that our car is fit for the journey and will not break down. Helping and counselling are, as I have said in previous chapters, responsible activities for which we need to maintain ourselves in a kind of peak form. The helper equivalent of a car breaking down due to poor maintenance is *burnout*.

'We often noticed that we had an argument every time that I had reconciled another couple. The couple had invested their violence in me, and I was investing it in my wife. I have always been aware my workshop provided a place where I could discharge my violence. Working on wood, steel or gold with hammer, saw or file, I could invest the violence which my patients had poured out on me in the consulting room.'

Paul Tournier: *The Violence Inside*, p.71

Burnout is the word we use to describe the damage we might do to ourselves if we don't get sufficient support. We may also of course, do damage to our helping relationships and/or the people we are trying to help if we don't get sufficient support. Since counselling takes a lot of effort, concentration and a clear mind, we need to be in peak form to be effective helpers or to do our best counselling. For many people being satisfied with our present level of effectiveness is not enough, we also want to continuously improve our abilities in counselling and helping.

So as helpers we need to do two things:
• Maintain ourselves to prevent burnout or damage to our clients.
• Develop and improve our helping abilities.

How can we as helpers or counsellors achieve these aims? Support for helpers and counsellors comes in many forms from informal, on-the-spot support to formal supervision required by a professional body. In the same way that the more time and effort you put into maintaining your car, the better and more reliably it runs, the more time and effort spent on establishing and maintaining your self as a helper and counsellor, the better off you will be.

Training and professional development.
You will have taken the first step to becoming a more effective helper by undertaking a basic introduction to counselling course. You will be helped to make up your mind about how far you wish to go with training. You will get an idea about the limits of counselling and the helping you can offer at different stages of training.

However far you proceed with training in counselling, you will find that your development as a helper never feels 'complete'. Practising professional counsellors attend training events to update their knowledge or gain new expertise in specialist areas. The BAC Journal, *Counselling* carries details of a wide range of training events open to all participants regardless of qualifications. Local 'alternative lifestyle' magazines also carry advertisements for events in your area.

Support you can give yourself
There are many contexts in which helping and counselling take place. The one common element in the various settings is *you*. There are some simple things we can all do to support our helping endeavours. The following are some suggested questions you could ask yourself before you start any helping activity:

• Make sure you're fit to help:
    • Are you physically well enough to give good quality help?
    • Have you been drinking or taking drugs?
    • Are you alert or are you feeling tired?
    ✍

• Prepare yourself to help:
    • Do you have the right amount of time to help?
    • Do you have the right kind of space you need to help? (Do you need it to be private, quiet or confidential?)
    ✍

• After you've done your helping:
  • How do you feel?
  • What do you need to do before you can continue work or go home? Talk to someone?
  • Have you made any notes that may be necessary?

✍

My rough rule of thumb is - if you're not fit to drive, you're not fit to help anyone properly. Similarly after a session helping or counselling you may need to sit for a moment to gather your thoughts or maybe talk to someone before you can carry on or drive home. Remember that counselling and helping take more out of you than you think and you may feel preoccupied with somone else's problems if you don't take a minute or two to recover your sense of who you are, and to separate yourself from them.

Basic support for basic helping

At this stage of training, you will be offering basic help and for this you will need to establish some basic support. It is not necessary to set up formal supervision sessions, although this may be done for you if you work for an agency or service as a volunteer.

There are some simple ways of getting the support you need to be an effective helper:

• Debriefing:
  This is when there is a set time after a critical incident, perhaps at work, for talking the incident through, getting any feelings off your chest. During the debriefing, normal work is suspended whilst the aftermath of the emergency is dealt with. In a helping setting this can be of use after a distressing session with a client, maybe one that has been verbally or physically abusive.

• Co-worker support:
  This happens when two helpers agree to pair up to support each other. They may make this a formal relationship where they agree to meet at set times, i.e. once a week. During these support sessions they may talk about the personal and learning issues that have arisen during their helping work that week. It can help if one takes the role of 'supporter' and the other the role of 'person supported'. This can stop the session becoming a general chat.

  Sometimes this co-worker support can be in the form of an agreement to be available in emergencies, i.e. perhaps being wiiling to be contacted at home on the phone to offload stress.

• Support groups:
  Sometimes, a number of helpers agree to get together to talk over the difficulties of their work. They don't have to come from the same place of work, indeed, sometimes it can be an advantage to talk to someone who is not a work colleague since they can give you a different perspective on a situation because they are not so closely involved.

• Support network:
  You may agree to exchange telephone numbers or addresses with a group of helpers. Then we offer 'spot support' if something

arises out of our helping work on the spur of the moment. This works well in rural or less well populated areas where people live a long way apart or where people don't have access to transport.

• Special training events:
Many services and agencies run special training events every month or two months where people get together to learn about a new or developing aspect of the helping professions. The discussions afterwards give opportunities for informal support or may help you set up one of the support systems mentioned above. There are several regional BAC branches which run events and meetings on a monthly basis. Contact BAC at their Rugby address for details of activities in your area.

Some groundrules for basic support
If you are called upon to support another helper whether they are a colleague and/or a friend, try following these rules. Don't be afraid to offer support; if you intend to be supportive by providing a safe environment, you won't go far wrong.

• Support and helping are very similar. Use what you know about helping in a counselling way to give support to other helpers.

• Use active listening skills to listen carefully to what the other person is saying.

• Don't be afraid if they get upset when they're talking. It's quite natural for helpers themselves to get upset when they need support .

Backup
So far I've been talking about support for helpers in terms of how to offload the feelings we all get when we have to listen to other people's troubles on a regular basis.

There is, however another kind of support which is invaluable, if not essential. I call it *backup*. You will know what backup is if you work for a service or agency such as The Samaritans. There they have more than one person on duty at most times and each volunteer on duty is backed up by a day leader - somone on call at home or work who can give information, advice, guidance and support to the volunteer if something crops up that's beyond their limits. Samaritans branches usually have backup from a local doctor who can help volunteers if the client has a problem which might have a medical element.

Backup is great if you've got it, but very difficult, if not impossible to organise if you're working or helping on your own. Perhaps you want to use your counselling-style at home with your family and friends, in your neighbourhood or at work. There's no need to feel completely isolated, since we have looked at ways of getting basic support. It is also possible to *feel* backed up even though you haven't any proper backup. There are plenty of professional helpers such as doctors and social workers who can back up any first-aid helping you might do.

When helping someone, you may decide that it's best if they get help from someone better qualified (see Chapter 6 What To Do When You Reach Your Limits) or you might want to help them get some detailed information about their problem. Here's a short list of possible steps to take:

• Find out who their GP is and how to get in touch.

• Do they have a social worker, home help or health visitor?

• The Citizen's Advice Bureau near you is another source of information, advice and backup.

✍ Other sources of backup in your area.

Supervision for professional counsellors

As I mentioned above, practising professional counsellors are required to be supervised by various codes of ethics and practice, e.g. British Association for Counselling Code of Ethics and Practice for Counsellors. I decided to look briefly at supervision for counsellors to give readers an idea of the responsibilities involved in being a counsellor and the safeguards in place to ensure that clients get the best quality help.

You may be familiar with the term 'supervisor' when used in other settings. For example a supervisor at work may be your line manager or someone who oversees or checks your work. Sometimes a supervisor is someone who takes overall responsibility for a job or chases the job's progress. Counselling supervision means none of these things.

• As a counsellor your supervisor should not be someone you work with. Your supervisor should not be your line manager.

• Your supervisor should not be someone you are very friendly with.

When either of the above situations arise, it is called a *dual relationship*, i.e. you have two relationships running alongside each other, a work or friendship alongside a supervision relationship. This can lead to conflicts of interest and when this happens either one or both of the relationships may be compromised.

• Your supervisor should be someone who is a qualified counsellor with some years experience of counselling, although it is not necessary for them to be more experienced than you.

• Your supervisor should be someone who can challenge your comfortable assumptions about your work.

'It is a breach of the ethical requirement for counsellors to practise without regular counselling supervision/consultative support.

Counselling supervision/consultative support refers to a formal arrangement which enables counsellors to discuss their counselling regularly with one or more people who have an understanding of counselling and counselling supervision/consultative support. It's purpose is to ensure that efficacy of the counsellor-client relationship. It is a confidential relationship.'

Code of Ethics and Practice for Counsellors, BAC (1992) Ammended AGM September 1993 par. B.3.1 & B.3.2.

Who is Counselling For? 9

For the purposes of this brief chapter, I would like to stand aside from the usual debate about what counselling is. Elsewhere in this book I have looked at some of the information and argument in this debate regarding counselling, counselling skills and psychotherapy. I have contributed to the debate by suggesting that there is another type of informed helping at a level below the counselling skills level which is a valid and honourable *basic helping* activity.

Rather than re-hash that debate yet again, I would rather offer a few illustrations of who seeks and receives counselling in the UK. How they do it and what is likely to happen. It is not intended to be a comprehensive list. As with other parts of this book, it aims to be both informative and a starting point for further exploration, aims that are, I believe, in harmony with an introductory course.

Why do people seek counselling-style helping?

Many people now accept that talking through problems is beneficial. The word *counselling* comes readily to the lips of anyone seeking such an opportunity to talk and be listened to. A glance at the notice board in your public library or a flick through the front of your telephone directory will give you an insight into the range of local problem-related counselling services available. It may seem all to obvious that counselling is for people with problems.

It may be less obvious that a growing number of people in this country seek counselling as a route to self-improvement. In a similar way to seeking self-improvement through yoga classes, sport, arts and crafts, adult education such as writing for pleasure, people seek self-improvement through counselling. Although this may seem to be a solitary and costly leisure activity, it needn't be. There are several peer-support networks around the country where people get together in pairs and larger groups to offer help and counselling to each other. The most well known of these networks are called *co-counselling communities*.

Embedded within this 'counselling-for-self-improvement' activity is a dimension of counselling and helping that is only recently getting the attention it deserves. That is the spiritual dimension. The search for self-improvement and self-fulfilment inevitably touches upon the spiritual side of humanness. Not only is this spiritual dimension present for the seeker, but also for the helper/counsellor. As William West(1994) commented recently at the British Psychological Society Division of Counselling Psychology Conference, forming helping and therapeutic relationships with people five days a week all year is a deeply spiritual process. Many helpers and those seeking help make direct links between helping and spiritual life by doing their helping in a religious context. Counselling fits well into many spiritual traditions.

Problem-centred helping and counselling

The term counselling sits quite comfortably alongside information, advice and guidance when it comes to thinking about helping strategies for problems. People in need do not care what the process is called, nor what comes along with it. However, most agencies offering information, advice and guidance will explicitly offer counselling, or acknowledge that counselling skills are used in the delivery of their other helping services.

Perhaps it is because we have a keener sense of the need for support at times of personal crisis and know what good helping is. Or perhaps it is because of the breakdown of support systems like the extended family in our society, that there has been an explosion of agencies and services offering support and counselling in the past 20 years. As seekers of help we have become accustomed to looking for, and more often than not finding, help tailored to our specific needs. Some of the critical life events that take us to counselling are listed below with a word or two of explanation.

Bereavement.

The one life-event which is universally accepted as a time when humans need support. Much work has been published on the grief process, how unresolved grief can lead to more serious damage and how counselling can help. Grief support and counselling is popular as a peer activity through organisations such as Cruse, and a specialism offered by many professional counsellors.

Unresolved grief can lead to much more complicated and long-lasting symptoms, so good support through bereavement is sometimes literally a life-saver and invariably improves the quality of life. The term 'grief and loss' can encompass the reaction to any significant loss in a person's life including becoming unemployed, having a limb amputated or separating from your spouse.

Relationships and Marriage.

The well deserved reputation for excellent counselling gained by the former National Marriage Guidance Council, now known as Relate, has done much to associate relationship problems with counselling in the minds of the general public. Many people turn to relationship counselling before the relationship breaks down, whilst some want support after the event.

Gay couples are catered for within Relate, by specialist gay counselling services and through professional counsellors in private practice. People form ethnic minorities with relationship problems have some, though limited, opportunities to get more culturally sensitive help from specific agencies.

HIV and AIDS.

It has for some time been a requirement that all those requesting an HIV test receive 'counselling' before the test and on hearing the results. The quality of the counselling offered was variable and an attempt to address the problem was made in the report of the BAC and Department of Health Joint Project on HIV Counselling by Tim Bond (1990).

The need for counselling and support related to HIV and AIDS is not limited to those that are HIV positive or suffering from AIDS. Partners, relatives and friends need support too along with people who worry that they might have been infected. Some people become excessively worried about AIDS or HIV infection, despite being known to be uninfected or at little or no risk, are called 'worried well' and can take up a lot of time and resources of AIDS advice agencies.

Because the history of the spread of the HIV infection in the UK and USA has been amongst gay men and IV drug users, most specialised agencies are oriented towards the needs of these groups. However, a growing number of people not in these groups are needing support. In some areas a befriending scheme exists where people that are HIV positive are befriended by a 'buddy'. There are a few opportunities for black and ethic minority people to get culturally sensitive help.

Victim Support.

Now officially the title of a national, government funded organisation with local branches, victim support can also mean the help and counselling offered to any victim of crime. There is a growing concern that victims of crime have had their needs neglected and the provision of such schemes attempts to redress that imbalance.

Counselling for shock is offered alongside more concrete help with form filling, insurance claims and other everyday things that need doing after traumatic crime. Local schemes do try to meet local demand for minority languages and cultural minorities.

Surviving Disasters.

Post-traumatic stress disorder, or PTSD is the term used to describe the very distressing after-effects suffered by people who have survived trauma such as disasters. The events at Hillsborough football ground, the fire at Kings Cross Station, aircrashes and other disasters have prompted the provision of specific post-trauma counselling.

Post-trauma counselling is specialised work and is offered to a wide range of people including, for example, building society staff after armed robberies and members of the emergency services who witness horrific scenes in the course of duty.

Anyone surviving a trauma; car crash, mugging, or witnessing horrific accidents is vulnerable to PTSD and should be encouraged to seek help, whether or not a specific scheme is offered. Post-trauma counselling is now offered as a specialism by counsellors in private practice.

Surviving Abuse and Rape.

Rape and abuse are sometimes looked upon as separate issues, but I have put them together here to indicate that the victims and survivors are mostly women who have been subjected to male violence. This reflects the pattern of provision of support, help and counselling which is frequently by women for women.

There has been an increase in the attention given to child sexual abuse recently and the national agency Childline is a point of first contact. Much long-term counselling work is done with the adult survivors of such abuse. This is specialist work and the effects of remembering past abuse are frequently very traumatic and debilitating. This group does include men and it is thought by some that the degree to which it affects men has been underestimated.

Local organisations, rape crisis centres and womens' groups should be able to give initial support and make referrals where necessary. There is limited specialist provision for men or ethnic minority groups.

Sex and Sexuality.

Sex and sexuality are in fact two different problem areas - 'Sexuality' usually refers to sexual orientation, i.e. heterosexual, bisexual, gay, lesbian. Sexuality also covers sexual attraction to children, cross-dressing, wanting to hurt or be hurt by others, having less usual objects of sexual desire such as items of clothing or machinery.

Our culture is not very flexible when it comes to accepting sexuality or sexual practices which differ from the perceived cultural norm of heterosexual sex. The problems that most people have regarding their sexuality arises from this societal or family pressure to 'be normal'. Some sexual practices are illegal, such as paedophilia (sex with children) which may make it difficult for an active paedophile to seek help to change.

There are specialist self-help/support groups both nationally and regionally that offer help for people wanting to explore, come to terms with or change their sexual orientation. A mixture of information, advice, group support and counselling may be available.

'Sex' refers to problems with 'normal' sexual functioning. Popular terms describing these problems are 'impotence' in men (including premature ejaculation) and 'frigidity' in women. The problems include a wide range of incomplete, absent or inappropriate sexual responses and cause great distress and shame to the sufferers.

Counselling approaches pioneered in the UK by the then National Marriage Guidance Council (now Relate) are effective in a large proportion of cases. This specialist area requires counsellors with specialist training. Some professional counsellors in private practice offer sexual dysfunction counselling.

Medical Conditions.

Illness is another crisis point in a person's life where support is needed, not only for the person themselves but also for their family. Many medical conditions have long-term debilitating effects and a wide range of support groups offering services from information, advice, guidance, counselling and befriending have grown out of the need for such support. From arthritis and asthma to tinnitus (noises in the ear) there are organisations offering help, sometimes on a local basis - some employ specialist counsellors.

Some NHS specialist areas employ counsellors, e.g. to give advice to amputees or prospective parents who may be worried about their chances of having a normal child.

Suicide and despair.

Probably the most famous telephone helping agency, The Samaritans was set up to listen to people who were so desperate that they may consider taking their own life. Samaritans branches offer listening and befriending and are reluctant to call their basic helping 'counselling'. Undoubtedly, many Samaritans volunteers are proficient in the use of counselling skills. Volunteers are trained, but remain anonymous so on-going helping relationships are difficult unless a client is 'befriended' by a more experienced volunteer.

A few Samaritans branches offer minority languages and a service which takes into account local ethnic groups.

Problem pregnancies.

Trained counsellors should be on hand to help women make the decision as to whether she wants to terminate a problem pregnancy or not. Counselling at this important decision-point was pioneered by the BPAS and is now commonplace in other agencies offering a similar service. Some other agencies are tied to a world view or religious view which makes a pre-judgement about the morality of terminations and so the counselling is likely to be less than neutral. Information and advice are available in addition to counselling.

Counsellors are trained by mainstream agencies like BPAS and do an excellent job often under great pressure of time. Some limited after-event support is available, but a client may have to go elsewhere for this. Information and sometimes help is available in minority languages, but there are powerful cultural issues in the area of pregnancy and women's rights.

Counselling at Work.

A small but increasing number of employers are offering help, support and counselling through the workplace. Whether the problem is work-related or of a more personal nature, employers are beginning to realise the cost effectiveness of counselling since research suggests that when counselling is provided, fewer days are lost due to sickness and stress.

The current trend is to offer Employee Assistance Programmes (EAPs) rather than permanent on site counsellors. These give different levels of service to different grades of employee. Most start with telephone support to be followed by face-to-face counselling only if absolutely necessary.

Counselling at your GP surgery.

An increasing number of GPs employ counsellors in their surgeries to offer help with a wide range of problems from bereavement through to eating disorders and drug dependency.

Some surgeries may have help and information in minority languages. The counsellors should be well qualified and available on an appointment only basis. Ask your GP for information.

Counselling in Education.

Colleges and Universities have been providing counselling for students for many years. It is often provided under the heading 'student services', 'student support' or 'advice and guidance'. Information and advice, as well counselling for a wide range of academic, financial and personal problems is usually available. It is usual for the service to be offered to both full and part-time students.

Counsellors are usually well qualified and available on an appointment basis, with some limited provision for emergencies. Limited effort is made to provide a culture-sensitive service and information in minority languages, even though higher education institutions attract overseas students in number.

Counselling in schools is less available. Some education authorities have policies to provide schools' counsellors but this tends to be the exception rather than the rule.

Counselling and Religion.

The word 'counsel' does have religious associations and many people seek help from their church, or community elders when life presents them with crises. Bereavement is a time when people naturally turn to priests for support and guidance.

People resident in the UK turn to many religions and it is not the case that counselling values are shared by all cultures and all faiths. The help offered by priests and elders may not be in harmony with the counselling values espoused in this book.

Support and self-help for Women, Lesbians, Gays, Disabled people, Ethnic minorities, Young people.

Several groups of people band together as self-help groups with political leanings because they experience societies attitudes towards them as oppressive. They may have a view that the particular problems experienced by individuals in the groups are better explained and solved by looking at the issues of oppression first or alongside the problems of the individual.

There is sometimes a culture clash between counselling approaches and political approaches, since some people believe that it is the oppressive system that should change, not the individuals within it. Counselling skills are nearly always used by people in such groups but may not be explicitly acknowledged.

For further information about any application of counselling in the UK you should find the following publication useful:

Counselling and Psychotherapy Resources Directory, published by The British Association for Counselling. It is updated annually and should be available from your college or local library. Copies can be bought direct from BAC. It contains contact numbers for all national and local counselling organisations, including specialist groups, ethnic minorities etc., along with individual counsellors and other useful information.

After completing an introductory course in counselling, you might be able to recommend counselling opportunities to relatives, friends and colleagues in need of help. This would, of course, include pointing them in the right direction for well qualified help, be it Relate, Childline or the local womens' group. It would not be appropriate to offer help yourself in any capacity other than a relative, friend or colleague.

If you would like to volunteer: First find out the names of the organisations that work in the area of your interest. Contact their national or local address, which you will find in the *Counselling and Psychotherapy Resources Directory* (see above). You will probably have to undergo training by the organisation concerned. Finally, check that you can make the time commitment required.

Who Does What in Helping?
Psychology, Counselling and Psychotherapy

10

Many people are puzzled by the confusingly complicated array of professionals offering services in the general field of psychological therapies, and it's growing by the day. The British Psychological Society has just announced the launch of its new Division of Counselling Psychology. So the choice is now between:

- Counsellor
- Psychotherapist
- Counselling Psychologist
- Educational Psychologist
- Clinical Psychologist
- Psychiatrist

What do they all do and who should we go to see or refer our clients to, and under what circumstances? Starting at the bottom of the list I will give a brief summary of the training and qualifications necessary, the type of clients seen and the type of treatment used for each of the professional groups above. One final word of caution, there will be differences within each professional group so all that I can attempt is a general set of guidelines for understanding this area. There will be exceptions to these general rules, and I hope the information stays current long enough to be useful.

Psychiatrist. It might have been sufficient a few years ago to say that a psychiatrist is a doctor who specialises in the treatment of mental illness and leave it at that. In recent years the medical profession has had to become more accountable and we want to know more about the qualifications and responsibilities of medical practitioners.

After qualifying as a doctor and gaining experience in general medicine, specialisation is the next step for medical students. Psychiatry is one of several specialisms such as general practice, surgery, paediatrics etc. It involves some years spent in full-time specialised psychiatry training. Look out for the following letters signifying higher qualifications in psychiatry:

DPM (Diploma in Psychiatric Medicine)
MRCPsych (Member of the Royal College of Psychiatrists)
FRCPsych (Fellow of the Royal College of Psychiatrists)
DM or MD (doctoral thesis) in a psychiatric subject.

However, any qualified doctor can call him or herself a psychiatrist if they undertake treatment of psychiatric patients, even if they have no specialist training at all.

The vast majority of psychiatrists work in NHS settings and will have patients referred to them by GPs or other healthcare professionals. Some psychiatrists will see fee-paying patients privately, though there will be little difference in the treatment. Psychiatrists are also usually on call at casualty departments, so reporting to casualty is a method of self-referral.

The typical caseload of a psychiatrists will include many people experiencing serious mental disturbances of either a temporary or more enduring type. Such serious disturbances often mean that the patient is thought to be a danger to themselves or others (although this is a contentious issue) or is incapable of looking after themselves. There is an increasing tendency to call for the support of a psychiatrist when all other options are exhausted.

The role of the psychiatrist is changing in the UK from someone who delivers treatment, to someone who manages a treatment plan. Their role is also invested with statutory powers such as prescribing drugs and authorising admission to or discharge from hospital.

Treatments used by psychiatrists reflect the medical history and tradition of psychiatry. They are more likely to use 'physical' treatments e.g. drugs and electroconvulsive therapy (ECT). Only medically qualified persons can prescribe such treatments. Psychiatrists are less likely to use 'talking therapies' themselves (possibly due to lack of time), although they may prescribe psychological treatment via a clinical psychologist or specialist nurse.

Psychologist. When used on its own, the title 'psychologist' has little meaning. In order to become a psychologist all that is really needed is a psychology degree (BA or BSc). Psychology is the study of the normal mental life and behaviour, mainly of human beings, but also of some animals where their behaviour can throw light on human behaviour. Being a psychologist in no way qualifies or prepares a person to offer help to those with any form of mental distress or disturbance.

Chartered Psychologist. Is the title used by someone who has a first degree in psychology, a further qualification or period of supervised training in a practical area of psychology, such as clinical, educational or counselling psychology, and been judged fit to practise psychology without supervision. Chartered Psychologists are members of the British Psychological Society (BPS) and abide by their own Code of Conduct with its attendant complaints procedure. Chartered Psychologists can use the letters *C Psychol* after their name. All Chartered Psychologists and a description of the services they offer can be found in the register of Chartered Psychologists, a copy of which can be found in your local public library.

Chartered Counselling Psychologist. Is a Chartered Psychologist specialising in counselling psychology and a member of the Division of Counselling Psychology. They will have a Diploma in Counselling psychology or have equivalent certified qualifications and experience. Counselling Psychologists can work in a variety of settings including private practice and will, according to the BPS, work with adults, groups, students and young people, families and couples, the elderly, in health and medical settings, in work settings and in community settings. Counselling psychologists will work using a range of counselling skills and methods that are informed by psychological knowledge and research.

Counselling Psychology is the most recent addition to the list of specialisms offered by BPS Chartered Psychologists, so there are not very many practising Counselling Psychologists around at the time of writing. A number are in private practice, and full details can be obtained from the BPS or from the Directory of Chartered Psychologists. Because of the small number, you are unlikely to be referred to one by your GP or anyone else. You would have to specifically ask or look for one yourself.

Chartered Clinical Psychologist. Clinical psychologists traditionally work in medical or mental health settings. They may have a further specialisation, e.g. in child clinical psychology. They practise a number of psychological assessment and treatment techniques such as psychological testing, behavioural therapies and helping people rehabilitate after brain injury or disease. Many use counselling-type relationship skills alongside the psychological therapies, but not all do. Their clients or patients are likely to be suffering from an acute or enduring mental illness, such as panic attacks, phobias, obsessive disorders, schizophrenia-like conditions, depression, etc.

Clinical psychologists have their own health service structure through which their services are delivered, usually managed by a District Clinical Psychologist. Referral to the clinical psychologist will be from your GP, Psychiatrist or other health service specialist. You may ask for a referral if you think a clinical psychologist would help, or you could find one that takes private clients in your locality.

Chartered Educational Psychologist. Psychologists working in educational settings or specialising in psychology related to education and children are called educational psychologists. They work mainly with children and adolescents up to the age of 19 and receive most referrals via the education system or parents. Their clients will be wanting help with a range of social and emotional problems which may manifest themselves through school, or academic and intellectual problems such as dyslexia and special learning needs.

Educational psychologists offer a range of assessments and treatments including counselling approaches, but also behavioural therapies, e.g. for bed wetting, and learning programmes or resource management for children with special learning needs. If a child is having problems at school, then the educational psychologist will probably use psychological testing to help diagnose the problem before applying specific treatments. They will also work with children in emotional difficulties, including court work if the child needs to be put in a place of safety.

Educational psychologists are usually employed by Local Education Authorities (LEA) and can be accessed through schools or directly by looking up the LEA or Schools' Psychological Service in the phone book. You can also have private consultations if you wish by finding a local Educational Psychologist in private practice.

Psychotherapist. To some extent the difference between psychotherapists and counsellors is as artificial as the difference between psychotherapy and counselling. It is not uncommon to find two people with identical qualifications and client caseloads, one of whom calls themselves a counsellor, whilst the other calls themselves a psychotherapist. By a similar token you may find the same person calling themselves both a counsellor and a psychotherapist (and sometimes a counselling psychologist too).

Laying aside any such problems, the United Kingdom Council for Psychotherapy (UKCP) is a professional body looking after the interests of psychotherapists and psychotherapy. It monitors standards of training, has a code of conduct and a register of practitioners. The UKCP works alongside other organisations such as BAC in the development of standards in therapeutic helping.

Psychotherapists work in a range of healthcare settings and in private practice. They employ a range of therapeutic techniques for helping clients. There are many different 'schools' or approaches in psychotherapy, but any competent therapist will explain the basis of the techniques that they use should you wish to know. There are specialisms within psychotherapy including child and family therapists, art and drama therapists.

If you feel that a psychotherapist can help, you should contact the UKCP for access to the register or ask your GP to refer you.

Counsellor Some years a go a friend of mine wrote a short article for a student magazine defining psychology. His conclusion was: 'Psychology is what psychologists do'. It might seem flippant to start with the statement: 'Counsellors are people who do counselling', but I fear it's going to be the closest I can get in a single statement.

There is no single route to being a counsellor, and there are many specialisms within counselling, bereavement counsellor, drugs counsellor, student counsellor, HIV/AIDS counsellor, etc. One distinguishing feature which may be helpful is that many counsellors are professional, that is they earn their living as a counsellor. This will usually indicate a degree of training and experience above that usually associated with being a volunteer or someone using counselling skills, *but not always*.

Minimum qualifications would be a Diploma in Counselling or equivalent. The BAC recognises a few Diploma courses which come up to agreed minimum criteria. Such courses will say 'BAC Recognised Course'.

Many counsellors will be members of BAC (therefore subject to the BAC Code of Ethics and Practice) and some will be BAC Accredited Counsellors (see below and page 100).

If you want to choose a counsellor working in private practice, there are helpful guidelines in the Counselling and Psychotherapy Resources Directory. I would reiterate the point made in the directory regarding word-of-mouth recommendation. A job well done is often the best way of choosing someone alongside checking out their qualifications and membership of a professional body. Do not apologise for being choosy.

BAC Accredited Counsellor. Being Accredited means that the counsellor has a certain level of training and experience that has been scrutinised by the BAC. Not all counsellors eligible for Accreditation have applied for this status.

The BAC and UKCP are working jointly on a register of counsellors and psychotherapists, but this may have changed by the time this book is published. If anyone wants further clarification or help they should contact one of the professional bodies concerned. Contact addresses for the British Association for Counselling, the British Psychological Society and United Kingdom Council for Psychotherapy can be found at the end of this book.

What Comes Next?

11

As you come to the end of this course there are several options open to you. Some people will have already decided what their next step is going to be. Others will not be so sure, nor even be sure what the next step *could* be. In Chapter 9 I wrote that some people seek counselling for self-development rather than to resolve a problem or in response to a crisis. So it is with counselling training. Some of you will have started this course with a view to increase your knowledge of helping processes, general understanding and self-awareness. Initially you may not have considered any career as a helper either paid or voluntary.

Similarly, the process of the course will have helped some of you to make the decision that counselling or helping in a counselling way is not for you. For those of you who have made this decision, I hope that you can be an advocate or ambassador for counselling after your experience on the course. By this I mean that you may be able to explain to friends, relatives and colleagues what a counselling way of helping is, that through your own experience you have found it to be helpful, principled, led by a body of knowledge; not just ad hoc. You may be able to point those around you in the right direction for good quality help should they wonder whether they need it, and that getting help at the right time improves the quality of our lives.

What options are available for those who wish to continue in their training in counselling? Firstly let me say that in my view, it is perfectly acceptable to pursue training in counselling to the next stage with the sole intention of developing self-awareness and self-improvement. I say this because I firmly believe that counselling skills are no more than good relationship skills and that I would support anyone seeking to improve their relationship skills. These more highly developed skills could then be used in a 'community' sense amongst one's family, friends and colleagues, and I think such 'communities' will be all the better for it.

The starting point - An Introduction to Counselling
The structure of counselling training varies slightly between the organisations offering training. There are usually three stages or levels, starting with basic introductory courses of between 10 and 30 hours spread over a weekend or several weeks of 2 - 3 hours per week. This book is written for this first level. Further training can be either full time or part time.

Part-time training: The next level of course is often called 'Certificate' level or 'Counselling Skills' level. Such courses are around 100 hours spread over one academic year (around nine months). Certificate courses use a range of written and practical assessment, though at this stage of training, the emphasis is usually on skills rather than academic criteria. The aim of these courses is to continue development of theory, self-awareness and counselling skills for those wishing to train as counsellors, whilst providing a genuine stopping off point for those wishing to train only in the use of counselling skills, but no further. So a certificate course would be of use to:

1. Teachers, nurses, social workers, youth workers and other helping professionals who were aiming to use counselling skills alongside their already established professional skills.

2. Those wanting to proceed to professional training at Diploma in Counselling level in order to be a counsellor.

3. Volunteers for advice and counselling agencies who want to continue development of their counselling skills beyond that offered by their basic agency training.

4. Anyone wanting to continue a 'counselling training' route to personal improvement and to use their counselling skills in the community.

Completion of a certificate course does not qualify someone to practise as a counsellor nor apply for a job as a counsellor under most circumstances. Certificates only qualify someone to use counselling skills.

A Diploma in Counselling is the professional practitioner level course. Diploma courses are of around 300 - 500 hours duration spread over 1 or 2 years. The BAC state in their Recognition of Counsellor Training Courses booklet that a course should be a minimum of 400 hours staff contact. Contact BAC for an updated list of BAC Recognised Courses. Diploma level courses should also require students to practise with bona-fide clients and have this work assessed in some way (often via audio-taped sessions). This practice is also supervised, either by course staff or external supervisors. Sometimes the cost of supervision is extra to the cost of the course. Assessment at Diploma level is rigorous and more academic than on skills courses. Here a balance between skills, academic understanding and personal development is sought so that a well-balanced practitioner is produced. Anyone applying for a Diploma in Counselling should realise that this level of training is demanding (and exciting and rewarding) and should set aside time during their week outside course contact time to see clients, for supervision, for reading and to complete assignments.

On completion of your diploma, you can practise as a counsellor and apply for jobs as a counsellor.

Full-time training: Some institutions offer full-time counsellor training and will take applicants who have completed an introductory course or have equivalent experience. Full-time courses are usually of 1 year's duration and are eligible for BAC Recognition.

Masters courses in counselling: There is now a number of higher degree courses in counselling studies. The emphasis is predominantly academic and often a research project or lengthy dissertation has to be completed. These courses are post-practitioner level and usually require a Diploma or equivalent as an entry qualification.

Accredited Counsellors: The BAC and Association for Student Counsellors or ASC (a Division of BAC) have grades of membership called Accredited Counsellor which means that the qualifications and experience of the counsellor meet certain criteria. These are, a Diploma or equivalent plus 450 hours of supervised counselling practice over a minimum three year period.

Endings

12

For some of us, endings of things just come and go along with the rest of everyday life; we are not very sensitive to them. For others, the end of something is an emotional time, a time to celebrate or to mark in some way. In counselling, endings have special meaning since the end of a helping relationship is symbolic of many moments of moving on in our lives.

The end of the course may also be a special time for course participants, perhaps marked by some exercises, at least to help you reflect on the experience of the course and review your learning on it. What do endings mean to you? What words and pictures come up for you?

```
ENDINGS

PARTING    DEATH    SORROW
FINISHED    GONE FOREVER    NO REGRETS
'YOU CAN NEVER GO BACK TO THE PAST'
LOSS    PAIN    GRIEF    SADNESS
'AS EACH DOOR CLOSES ANOTHER ONE
OPENS'
GOODBYE    MOVING ON TO BETTER THINGS

✍ .......... ............
```

The flipchart above is the last from our imaginary group. How do their responses fit in with your own? The end of the course is the end of the life of the group, the end of the relationships in the group as you knew them. Of course, some relationships may continue beyond the end of the course; you may have made new friends whom you will continue to see after the course or some of you may have decided to continue your training and will meet up with new people on the next course. It is easy to see endings as new beginnings or transitions from one state to another offering new and different opportunities.

How we handle endings on the course may reflect the way we feel about endings in our lives. Some may dread endings and put off thinking about them, others may eagerly look forward to them - impatient to move on to the next thing. You might also have a sense of the timing of endings; do they feel right and natural - has the course come to its natural end? Or does it feel too soon and that you are unprepared for the end? Are any of these familiar to you? What other endings can you remember, and how did you feel about them? Here are some to get started:

• Last day at school.
• Separation from spouse or ending a long-term relationship.
• Someone close to you dying.
• Moving house.

These endings may seem to have something in common with the changes we looked at in Chapter 3. Endings *are* change in the sense that they signal a change point that is inescapable. Some changes are gradual, but an ending or transition has a fixed moment. Sometimes we try to extend the ending by having a false ending before the 'real' one or by putting the ending off or by trying to recreate the way things were before the ending. For example, when someone close to us dies, we might want things to be the way they were - to bring that person back, or if we have a relative who is terminally ill, we begin the grieving process before they die (called anticipatory grieving).

If endings are such strong symbolic events for us, we must be ready to pay them special attention in the helping relationships we have. The people we are helping may have strong feelings about the end of the helping relationship:

• They may feel relief and want to get away from the 'old them' that the helping relationship reminds them of.

• They may want to hang on to the security of the helping relationship because they think they can't cope on their own.

The way we conduct ourselves as helpers in the final stages of a helping relationship will have an effect upon those we are trying to help. We must have an awareness of the meanings that endings have for us and not let our own meanings get in the way of our helping.

The end of the course provides us with an opportunity to experience some feelings about endings, past and present, enabling us to look at our patterns of behaviour. How will you end the relationships with the people on your course?

Reviewing our learning

I've deliberately written 'our learning', because, as you may remember, I started this book by saying that it would be better if I could form a relationship through the pages with you, the reader. Now the end of the book is here, I am aware that it is an ending for me. An end to sitting in front of my word processor, a sense of relief and some anxiety because I'm not sure how the book will be received. What have I learned? I like to ask the following simple questions to help review my learning at the end of courses. You could try it too.

• What have I learned about counselling?
• What have I learned about myself?
• What would I add to improve the experience and my learning?
• What would I remove to improve the experience and my learning?
• What will I do differently from now on?

✍ *You might like to make this the final entry in your journal.*

'This is not the end. It is not even the beginning. But it is, perhaps, the end of the beginning.'

Winston Churchill Nov. 1942.

Glossary

Active listening Paying close attention to all of the signals (including non-verbal communication) that convey meaning given off by the person being helped.

Affect The psychiatric and psychological term for any experience of feeling or emotion.

Anxiety Feeling of unexplained dread or impending disaster often distinguished from fear which is said to be the natural response to a clear and present danger.

Avoidance A defence mechanism in which situations, activities or objects that recall or represent painful events are avoided.

Befriending The provision of quality support of a 'friendly' nature intended to lessen a person's sense of personal or social isolation.

Behaviour therapy A form of psychotherapy which focuses on modifying faulty or unwanted behaviour rather than basic changes in personality.

Boundaries Boundaries are the limits which help define an activity by creating a space within which the activity can take place.

Clarifying Checking by paraphrasing and reflection that the client's meaning has been understood, and seeking the client's agreement with your understanding of what they have been saying.

Client-centred A way of working in counselling that puts the client at the centre of the activity, and has the belief that the client knows best how to solve their problems. Developed by Carl Rogers; now called Person-Centred.

Cognition A general psychological term for all forms of knowing or thought processes.

Cognitive therapy A psychotherapeutic approach based on the concept that emotional problems are the result of faulty ways of thinking and distorted attitudes towards oneself and others.

Congruence See Genuineness.

Core conditions The essential conditions identified by Carl Rogers without which helpful change cannot take place.

Defence mechanism A psychological strategy employed to protect the individual from unpleasant or harmful forces.

Eclectic counselling Any counselling theory or practice that incorporates and combines doctrines, findings and techniques selected from diverse theoretical systems.

Empathy One of Carl Rogers' core conditions. The ability to sense the client's world *as if* it were your own, without losing the 'as if' quality.

Ethics Moral code or rules of conduct.

Genuineness One of the core conditions. It means being without 'front or facade'; being your real self in a helping situation, rather trying to be the 'expert'. This involves the acknowledgement of your feelings as they arise.

Gestalt therapy A form of psychotherapy first developed by Fritz Perls in which the central focus is on the client's "here and now" functioning and relationships, as opposed to investigation of past experiences and developmental history.

Hidden meaning Linked to Freud's ideas that actions have unconscious motivations and therefore a meaning that is not available to our conscious mind.

Humanism An outlook or system of thought in which human interests and dignity are valued rather than divine or supernatural matters.

Identification The process of associating one's self closely with other persons and assuming their characteristics or views.

Manipulation Behaviour designed to exploit or control others.

Motivation The process of initiating, sustaining and directing psychological or physical activities; the 'reason' for behaviour.

Non-directive An approach to counselling and psychotherapy, in which the client leads the way by expressing her own feelings, defining her own problems, interpreting her own behaviour, whilst the therapist sets up a permissive atmosphere and clarifies the client's ideas rather than directing the process. Although credited with developing the approach, Carl Rogers did not like the term.

Non-judgemental warmth See UPR.

Paraphrasing Summarising in few words what a person has just said to check understanding and to convey your attention.

Projection A defence mechanism in which unacceptable impulses are attributed to others or personal failures are blamed on others.

Psychodynamic General term for approaches to therapy and counselling heavily influenced by the work of Feud, although most such approaches have undergone significant development and owe just as much to the work of other influential figures such as Jung, Klein, etc.

Rational Emotive Therapy A therapeutic approach developed by Albert Ellis which concentrates upon the way we control our feelings and behaviour by irrational thoughts.

Referral The situation where a client or person being helped either moves on to another helper or comes to you from another helper.

Reflection At its most basic this involves reflecting back the other person's utterances as if in a mirror. It is used to convey empathy and as a check of understanding and to convey your undivided attention.

Schizophrenia A serious mental 'illness' associated with symptoms of disordered and confused thinking, inappropriate affect, delusions, hallucinations and acute anxiety.

Self-actualisation A humanist idea. According to Abraham Maslow it is the "full use and exploitation of talent, capacities, potentialities".

Stimulus In general, any event or situation, internal or external, that elicits a response from a person or organism.

Structuring Establishing the often unspoken 'rules' or boundaries of a relationship. In a helping relationship, this rule-setting or structuring is quite deliberate and may even take the form of some sort of contract.

Supervision The support necessary for all professional counsellors, usually from someone who has a similar background and who has no other relationship with the counsellor.

Symbol Any object, figure or image in our mind that represents something else.

Transactional analysis A form of dynamic group or individual therapy originated by Eric Berne, which focuses on characteristic interactions which reveal internal 'ego states' and the 'games people play' in social situations.

Transference Concept used in psychodynamic psychotherapy: the projection upon the therapist of unconscious feelings and wishes originally directed toward important individuals, such as parents, in the client's childhood.

Unconditional positive regard (UPR) Being able to accept the client totally as a worthwhile human being worthy, therefore, of respect; in effect, separating them from their behaviour. And being able to convey that unconditional respect with genuine warmth.

Useful Addresses

Advice, Guidance, Counselling and Psychotherapy Lead Body Secretariat 40A High St, Welwyn, Herts, AL6 9EQ.

British Association for Counselling 1 Regent Place, Rugby, Warwickshire, CV21 2PJ.

British Psychological Society St Andrews House, 48 Princess Road east, Leicester, LE1 7DR.

United Kingdom Council for Psychotherapy Regent's College, Inner Circle, Regent's Park, London NW1 4NS.

References

Tim Bond (1990) *HIV Counselling : Report on National Survey and Consultation 1990.* BAC & Dept. Health.

Claude Bristol (1985) *The Magic of Believing,* a Fireside Book published by Simon & Schuster.

British Association for Counselling, *Counselling & Psychotherapy Resources Directory,* (Published annually).

British Association for Counselling, *Code of Ethics and Practice for Counsellors* (1992 Ammended AGM 1993).

British Association for Counselling, *Code of Ethics and Practice for Counselling Skills* (1989).

British Association for Counselling, *Code of Ethics and Practice for the Supervision of Counsellors* (1988).

British Association for Counselling, *Code of Ethics and Practice for Trainers* (1985).

British Association for Counselling, *Definition of Terms in Use with Expansion and Rationale,* (1991).

British Association for Counselling, *The Recognition of Counsellor Training Courses,* Second Edition (1990).

British Psychological Society, *Directory of Chartered Psychologists,* (Published annually).

Dryden, W. and Spurling, L. eds (1989) *On Becoming a Psychotherapist,* London: Routledge.

Egan, G., (1994) *The Skilled Helper - A Problem-Management Approach to Helping.* Brooks/Cole.

Eysenck, H.J. (1953) *Uses and Abuses of Psychology,* Pelican published by Penguin Books Ltd.

Marilyn Ferguson, (1981) *The Aquarian Conspiracy,* Routledge.

Friends, Religious Society of, *Questions & Counsel,* London Yearly Meeting 1988 No16.

Hannah Green, (1972) *I Never Promised You a Rose Garden.* Pan. (1964 Gollancz)

Hjeller, L.A. and Ziegler, D.J., *(1981) Personality Theories - Basic Assumptions, Research and Applications,* McGraw-Hill.

Russell Hoban, (1975) *Turtle Diary,* Picador, published by Pan Books.

Edgar N. Jackson, (1978) *The Many Faces of Grief,* SCM.

Jung, C.G. (1954) *The Practice of Psychotherapy* Vol 16 of The Collected Works. London: Routledge & Keegan Paul.

Longman Dictionary of Psychology and Psychiatry, (1984), Longman.

Maeder, Thomas, (1989) *Children of Psychiatrists and Other Psychotherapists.* New York: Harper & Row.

Richard Nelson-Jones, (1993) *Practical Counselling and Helping Skills (3rd edn),* Cassell.

Ann Oakley, (1985) *Taking it Like a Woman,* Flamingo (Fontana Paperbacks)

Boris Pasternak, (1988) *Doctor Zhivago,* Harper Collins.

Carl Rogers, (1961) *On Becoming a Person,* Constable.

Carl Rogers, (1978) *Carl Rogers On Personal Power - Inner strength and its revolutionary impact,* Constable.

Natalie Rogers, (1980) *Emerging Woman - A Decade of Midlife Transitions,* Santa Rosa: Personal Press.

Janice Russell, Graham Dexter and Tim Bond (1992) *Differentiation Between Advice, Guidance, Befriending, Counselling Skills and Counselling,* Advice, Guidance and Counselling Lead Body.

Pete Sanders, (1993) *An Incomplete Guide to Using Counselling Skills on the Telephone,* Manchester: PCCS.

Secord, P.F. and Backman, C.W., (1974) *Social Psychology.* Tokyo: McGraw-Hill.

Brian Thorne, Psychotherapy and Counselling: The Quest for Differences, in *Counselling* Vol.3 No.4 (December 1992).

Paul Tournier, (1978) *The Violence Inside*, tr Edward Hudson. SCM.

Morris West, (1963) *Shoes of The Fisherman*, Heinemann.

William West, (1994) *A Study of the Relationship Between Counselling/Psychotherapy and Healing: first findings*, presentation at the BPS Counselling Psychology Conference.

Steve Williams, (1993) *An Incomplete Guide to Referral Issues for Counsellors*, Manchester: PCCS.

Winnicott, D.W. (1971) *Therapeutic Consultations in Child Psychiatry*, London: Hogarth Press.

LYRICS

Robert Smith: **Boys Don't Cry**, from the Album *'Staring at the Sea-The Singles'* by The Cure: Fiction Records.

Bjork Gudmundsdottir, Nellee Hooper and Antonio Carlos Jobim: **Human Behaviour**, from the album *'Debut'* by Bjork: One Little Indian Records.

David Byrne & Brian Eno: **Once in a Lifetime**, from the album *'Remain in Light'* by The Talking Heads: Sire Records.

David Couse: **I am Afraid**, from the album *'I am the Greatest'* by A House: EMI Records.

Further Reading

If you do not intend to continue your training in counselling but are still interested in this area:
Richard Nelson-Jones, (1990) *Human Relationship Skills (2nd edition)*, Cassell.

If you use counselling skills on the telephone in the course of your job or do telephone helpline work, either paid or as a volunteer:
Pete Sanders, (1993) *An Incomplete Guide for Using Counselling Skills on the Telephone*, PCCS.

If you are going to continue training on a certificate or counselling skills course:
Alan Frankland and Pete Sanders, (1995) *Next Steps in Counselling - A Students' Companion for Certificate and Counselling Skills Courses*, PCCS (in press for January 1995)

If you want to read more about specific counselling approaches (these are certificate-diploma level books, but quite easy to read):
Gerard Egan's approach:
Sue Culley, (1990) *Integrative Counselling in Action*, Sage.
Carl Rogers' approach:
Dave Mearns and Brian Thorne, (1988) *Person-Centred Counselling in Action*, Sage.